Working with Trauma

New Imago: Series in Theoretical, Clinical, and Applied Psychoanalysis
Series Editor: Jon Mills
Canadian Psychological Association

New Imago: Series in Theoretical, Clinical, and Applied Psychoanalysis is a scholarly and professional publishing imprint devoted to all aspects of psychoanalytic inquiry and research in theoretical, clinical, philosophical, and applied psychoanalysis. It is inclusive in focus, hence fostering a spirit of plurality, respect, and tolerance across the psychoanalytic domain. The series aspires to promote open and thoughtful dialogue across disciplinary and interdisciplinary fields in mental health, the humanities, and the social and behavioral sciences. It furthermore wishes to advance psychoanalytic thought and extend its applications to serve greater society, diverse cultures, and the public at large. The editorial board is comprised of the most noted and celebrated analysts, scholars, and academics in the English speaking world and is representative of every major school in the history of psychoanalytic thought.

Titles in the Series

Working with Trauma

Lessons from Bion and Lacan

Marilyn Charles, PhD

JASON ARONSON
Lanham • Boulder • New York • Toronto • Plymouth, UK

Published by Jason Aronson
A wholly owned subsidiary of Rowman & Littlefield
4501 Forbes Boulevard, Suite 200, Lanham, Maryland 20706
www.rowman.com

10 Thornbury Road, Plymouth PL6 7PP, United Kingdom

British Library Cataloguing in Publication Information Available

Library of Congress Cataloging-in-Publication Data

The hardback edition of this book was previously cataloged by the Library of Congress as follows:

Charles, Marilyn.
Working with trauma : lessons from Bion and Lacan / Marilyn Charles.
p. cm. — (New Imago: series in theoretical, clinical, and applied psychoanalysis)
Includes bibliographical references and index.
1. Psychoanalysis—Case studies. 2. Psychic trauma. I. Title.
RC509.8.C43 2011
616.8917—dc23
2011037096

ISBN: 978-0-7657-0680-5 (cloth : alk. paper)
ISBN: 978-0-7657-1006-2 (pbk. : alk. paper)
ISBN: 978-0-7657-0682-9 (ebook)

♾™ The paper used in this publication meets the minimum requirements of American National Standard for Information Sciences—Permanence of Paper for Printed Library Materials, ANSI/NISO Z39.48-1992.

Printed in the United States of America

Contents

Foreword

Marilyn Charles's book offers a privileged invitation into the intimacy of her work with her patients. Therapy is an act of imagination for both patient and therapist. More precisely, the impasses of which Marilyn speaks so eloquently in this book represent a failure of imagination on the part of patients who have experienced exquisite difficulties in their lives. The paradox, of course, is that while our patients come to us with literally unimaginable difficulties, we too suffer from failures of imagination and the difficulties of our patients can stoke our very own fears of breakdown.

We can increase our capacities for our work by expanding the repertoire of metaphors that are available to us so that patient difficulties beyond the realm of our everyday experience, or patient difficulties that awaken our own terrors, are speakable. W. R. Bion, Jacques Lacan, and Donald Winnicott, who are invoked regularly in the pages of this book, represent just such metaphorical companions. As Marilyn notes, repeatedly, we need to figure out how we might be of use to our patients, and her book is rich in examples of how our receptive and metaphorizing capacities are crucial to creating the kind of respectful engagement and the kind of narrativing possibilities that can cause a person at an impasse to find a way to start living their story anew.

Readers familiar with the writings of Bion, Lacan, and Winnicott will derive a special pleasure in entering the intimate space of Marilyn's case conceptualization and the rich opportunities it offers each of us to extend our own metaphoric incorporation of the wisdom of these great thinkers, as well as Marilyn's own original thinking. For people new to these thinkers, Marilyn's book provides an invitation to join the dialogue in a way that preserves the richness and complexity of their thought, and illustrates how, in dealing with a particular patient's difficulties, these powerful ideas can serve as metaphors that animate our imaginations and our own unconscious, so that we may, in turn animate our patients, to assist them, in the words of Davoine & Gaudillière, whom Marilyn also invokes, to turn into existence zones of non-existence.

I will leave to the reader the pleasure of discovering the ways in which Marilyn weaves theoretical ruminations, compelling clinical material, and honest self-reflexivity in the service of attempting to be useful to her patients—in struggling to become a good enough therapist for each one. What I will note, however, is how, following Lacan, she returns regularly to the ethical imperative of the work, an ethic of respect, existential presence—being without memory or desire—and a respect for the unconscious strivings of both patient and therapist, which are what make psychoanalysis as clinical practice so compelling.

As a research affiliate in the Psychosis Lab at the Austen Riggs Center I have been privileged to sit around a table with Marilyn and others for the past couple of years and I have been in awe at the depth of compassion, creativity, and human respect that are at the core of Marilyn's being as a therapist and as a person. I have learned a tremendous amount in the process, and now, with this book, Marilyn extends a lovely invitation to you, the reader, to join this conversation too.

Michael O'Loughlin
Adelphi University

Acknowledgments

I am grateful to my students, colleagues and, most of all, my patients, without whom this book would not have been possible. This is a profession in which we learn from our experience, and that learning is the stuff of which lives are made.

I particularly appreciate the time and attention of Julia Brown, Heather-Ayn Indelicato, Devon King, and Sandra Ullmann, whose thoughtful readings and support of the manuscript in progress were invaluable.

Prologue

The master breaks the silence with anything—with a sarcastic remark, with a kick start. That is how a Buddhist master conducts his search for meaning, according to the technique of *zen*. It behooves the students to find out for themselves the answer to their own questions. The master does not teach *ex cathedra* a ready made science: he supplies an answer when the students are on the verge of finding it.

This kind of teaching is a refusal of any system. It uncovers a thought in motion—nevertheless vulnerable to systematization, since it necessarily possesses a dogmatic aspect. . . . Our task, here, is to reintroduce the register of meaning. (Lacan, 1988, p. 1)

This book is written for those of you who are passionately devoted to becoming good clinicians and are drawn towards psychoanalytic theory and practice because you sense that there are useful insights there but have been inhibited by language barriers. This volume is intended as a sequel to *Learning From Experience: A Guidebook for Clinicians* (Charles, 2004a), an introduction to psychodynamic practice in which I translated ideas from object relations theory that are clinically useful but not easily accessible in the language of the original presentation. In the present volume, I address ideas that I have found to be fundamental when working with more severely traumatized individuals, with the hope that you will find them clinically relevant. Rather than offering more lengthy case vignettes, I will use clinical moments when possible. I hope that these moments will be sufficiently familiar to enable you to consider how you might or might not apply the highlighted concepts in your own practice.

As those of you know who are familiar with that previous text, my roots are in object relations theory, most particularly in the works of Winnicott, Klein, and Bion, whose conceptualizations I have found vital to my ability to be useful to my patients. I had always been drawn to the obvious brilliance of Lacan, having the sense of clinical insights tantalizingly out of reach. It wasn't until I encountered clinicians from the GIFRIC (Groupe interdisciplinaire freudien de recherches et d'interventions clinique et culturelles) group in Québec, however, that I finally found the core clinical utility of Lacan. These clinicians founded the "388," a highly successful clinic in which they use conceptualizations from Lacan to inform the psychoanalytic treatment of psychotic young adults. That encounter fundamentally changed my thinking and my practice, and has informed my teaching and supervision as well.

In this volume, I will discuss these fundamental insights of Lacan that I have found important to have in mind when working with more severely disturbed individuals. In addition, we will also consider insights gleaned from Bion's work with psychotic patients. As we do so, we will recognize that Winnicott, in his own way, was often pointing to similar insights. Looking through multiple lenses helps us obtain a clearer glimpse of the clinical moment each theorist was addressing and perhaps helps us to be more respectful of our own ways of managing such moments. In this way, I will offer ways of thinking and of being with individuals who have been fundamentally destabilized by trauma, hoping that these ideas will help you to keep your bearings through the difficult—but rewarding—work required.

Chapter One

Introduction

Psychoanalysis finds itself at a crossroads where the momentum of the past no longer seems sufficient to carry this rich and clinically useful body of knowledge into the future. Training institutions, once proudly and profoundly psychodynamic, now run the risk of losing touch with their roots as they try to 'keep up with the times' and accommodate to the demands of a changing world. In our haste to move forward, we risk losing sight of exactly those factors that have kept psychoanalysis alive as an important therapeutic endeavor despite repeated reports of its demise.

We live in an age of quick fixes that lend themselves to 'practical,' pragmatic solutions to complex problems (see Charles, 2008, 2009). Some problems are well fixed in such fashion but others are not. For those individuals whose problems are not so easily allayed, the failure to find relief can seem to mark a *personal* failure, obscuring the *structural* aspects that may be keeping the problem in place (LaCapra, 1999). The failure to appreciate the larger social contexts in which an individual's problems are embedded not only makes it more difficult to address those structural problems but also increases the sense of hopelessness, helplessness, despair, and isolation that can accompany severe problems in living.

The specific causes of severe and persistent psychological dis-ease remain obscure and yet we do know that stress exacerbates internal vulnerabilities, and that chronic stress ravages us physiologically as well as psychologically. Often, the very 'cures' offered to relieve such debilitating stress offer only partial relief and do so at a cost in terms of side effects and also in terms of the labels assigned to the sufferer (Whitaker, 2010). Although the medical model has helped us to organize our thinking so that we are better able to recognize constellations of problems that tend to co-occur, one price has been the reification of the categories thus created, inviting us to lose sight of the person and his or her unique experience. Losing sight of the human being who is in trouble may be so destructive that whatever we offer at that point may not be terribly valuable to the individual who is fighting to obtain respect for a selfhood that is fragile, unstable, and in desperate need of support. I think, for example, of a young man for whom labels critically limited his ability to engage in conversation. Although he knew that his perceptions had been distorted by a traumatic experience, calling this distortion a "delusion" felt to him like a denial of the enormity of what had befallen him. He could agree that the experience was psychotic but not that it was a delusion. Failing to take into account the meanings *for the other person* of whatever we are saying or doing can retraumatize the very person we are intending to assist. Attending to the subjective experience of the other has been a hallmark of psychoanalytic psychotherapy. Lacan deepens the challenge by noting how easily one's authority as a Subject can be diverted by deference to the Other. We will take up this central dilemma in Chapter 2, as we consider how we might assist our patients in recognizing *their* desires rather than imposing our own.

In a study specifically focusing on interactions between mental health professionals and individuals who have been diagnosed with psychosis, my colleagues and I found that meaning can be highly constrained by the interpersonal engagement in the moment (Charles, Clemence, Newman, & O'Loughlin, 2011). A sensitive interviewer could afford the interviewee sufficient closeness or distance by paying close attention. The importance of attending to ways in which the patient stumbles or retreats will be taken up in Chapter 3. Tracking the person in this way could pull a seemingly dull or incoherent individual into cogency, whereas insensitivity to cues could result in muteness, incoherence, or dull and minimal or routinized responses (See Chapter 11). If taken seriously, this research evidence may be useful in helping us to evaluate treatment options. A humanistic approach can be an important safeguard when weighing research, particularly given the current trend to *overvalue* quantitative data and to *undervalue* qualitative data. Whereas evidence from randomized control studies tends to affirm the medical model of mental disorder and the efficacy of shorter term treatments, evidence also continues to mount regarding the value of more intensive long-term therapy and the fundamental importance of human connections in our work with more severely disturbed individuals (Charles, 2009).

Biological studies of kindling effects show how unrelieved trauma can be exacerbated over time, leading to greater distress and less resilience. 'Kindling' refers to situations in which the repetition of a stimulus accumulates over time, making it more likely that the effect will occur. Ethnographic and transgenerational studies show how suffering that is insufficiently understood or relieved not only increasingly affects the *individual* over time but also can be passed along the generations.

Disruptions that occur at the social level—such as forced migration, war, poverty, sudden deaths, or environmental disasters—may tax not only the individual but also the family and/or community in which he is embedded.

The Holocaust literature has shown that attempts to just 'move on' without coming to terms with the enormity of the trauma may have devastating effects on successive generations who may not even know what they are mourning. Mourning remote losses such as these is problematized when one knows that the suffering of previous generations was certainly greater than one's own in pragmatic terms. And yet, it is often the trauma that] *6* has been passed along through the generations that is most insidious. Coming to grips with the story that underlies the symptoms of trauma can be an important part of healing, as we rediscover whatever has been left unknown or unintegrated precisely because of its traumatic impact (Davoine & Gaudilliére, 2004).

When we work with traumatized individuals, our empathic resonance invites us to share deeply in their suffering. This is a difficult challenge to] *7* sustain over time. As we sit with the utter horror that has so waylaid another human being in their life journey, we may feel overwhelmed, unprofessional, or as though we are not doing good work. The urge to designate that person as Other can be quite compelling; to believe that there is some fundamental difference between us that would mark an unbreachable barrier between the I and thou that Buber (1958) marks as the essential relation of subject-to-subject. It can be easier to sit with some poor unfortunate person who has a mental disorder rather than to confront the terrible fact that 'there but for the grace of God, go I.' Such is the urge to designate otherness that we can experience relief from designating traumatized individuals as 'psychotic' or 'character-disordered' or, perhaps more benignly, as suffering from PTSD rather than more pointedly recognizing the toxic effects of suffering itself on us all.

Current western medical practice invites us to try to relieve suffering as quickly and conveniently as possible, and we have developed an arsenal of drugs to help us wage this war against 'mental illness' and seemingly intolerable distress. At times, drugs may alleviate the distress to some extent but often they do not, and psychiatric medications are not benign. Even when they provide relief, the toll they take can be very high (Whitaker, 2002). The search for the 'right drug' can become an end in itself, inviting increased frustration without dealing with the underlying problems in living that have developed over time (Mintz & Belnap, 2006).

The failure to thrive is itself a problem, having many meanings for the individual, particularly in cultures where we have the idea that if we 'just worked hard enough' everything would be ok. Succeeding in one area while failing to achieve other developmental milestones not only causes problems in our relationships with others but also affects our ideas about ourselves.

Often, the failure becomes a source of shame that marks an internal deficit to be hidden rather than an obstacle to be managed or overcome. We will take up the subject of shame in Chapter 4.

For the individual who has fundamentally lost his or her way, the problems become multi-layered, so that it can be difficult to distinguish between cause and symptom. At the extreme, trauma makes it difficult to make use of our own internal signals, thereby not only making us a stranger to ourselves but also making us unable to adaptively attend to and relieve our own distress. Notably, the failure to effectively learn basic self-regulatory functions seems to be at the core of most severe psychopathology. If I cannot recognize my own needs and feelings, I am at the mercy of whatever is offered, including others' definitions of me. If I am quite desperate, I may be willing to take almost anything that might offer some respite and, if I have internalized a critical parental representation, I may use potentially useful treatments in self-destructive ways.

This type of self-destructive use of treatment options has been found with medications (Mintz & Belnap, 2006) and also with ECT (Charles & Clemence, 2010), at times with devastating consequences. ECT, for example, is contraindicated with certain personality disorders because the harm can outweigh potential benefits. There have been cases in which individuals have sought out repeated series of ECT treatments in spite of their failure to obtain benefit. At times, these actions can be well understood in relation to the life history. Failure to recognize the dynamic meanings can be devastating. Some of these cases, for example, have resulted in neurological impairment that did not relieve over time.

In my work with individuals who have become severely waylaid in their lives, I have been caught at times between very different standards regarding what could or should be done about such problems (Charles, 2008; 2009). I have found that people may have very different experiences of medications or techniques at any given point in time, and so I try to encourage patients to become educated consumers, paying close attention to information offered by experts and even closer attention to the impact on their minds and bodies of whatever offerings they decide to try. I find that if I am respectful of the various considerations the person encounters, I can be a useful resource while they think through the various short- and long-term consequences of their choices. In this process, I hope that they can also learn to recognize and more reflectively consider their own ambivalent motivations. The extent to which reflective function is being encouraged or discouraged in moment by moment interactions in the consulting room is always an important element for the clinician to consider, and yet training in making these types of discriminations is rarely explicitly taught. Fonagy and his colleagues are beginning to address this training deficit by illustrating ways in which mentalization is a core aspect of any therapeutic relationship (Allen, Fonagy, & Bateman, 2008).

One offering that has been shown to be effective over time in relieving some of the suffering associated with severe trauma is psychoanalytic psychotherapy. That is the work I will be discussing in this volume, as I try to translate for you some key conceptualizations from Bion and Lacan that I find useful in working with more severely distressed individuals. Bion and Lacan were writing at approximately the same point in time. Although they each developed a different language for discussing their work with psychotics and other severely disturbed individuals, the underlying principles were in some ways remarkably similar.

Bion (1977) often uses metaphor when pointing to a complex clinical fact. His idea of *bi-nocular vision* highlights the usefulness of having two different vantage points from which to look at the same subject. Bion notes that although we can see with either eye, it is only by putting the two eyes together that we can make use of the added dimension of depth perception. Matte-Blanco (1975) notes the tendency to oversimplify when we come up against the limits of mind and imagination. Recognizing this tendency can, perhaps, help us to open our minds when we come up against these limits. At the point, for example, when I can notice that my patient and I are stuck in part because I have closed my mind to his perspective, I can, perhaps, step back a bit and try to look at the 'clinical facts' in a way that includes the patient's vantage point along with my own. I have noticed that this space tends to close down when I am dealing with a difficult problem that is not easily solved and from which the patient earnestly desires relief. In such moments, it can be easy to come to a simplistic solution that only appears tenable because I have one eye shut to the complexities of what the patient is revealing to me. We will consider this tendency to turn a blind eye in Chapters 5 and 6.

Psychoanalytic clinical work is grounded in the idea that both people are essential to the encounter. Being able to view complex phenomena from more than one vantage point helps to enlarge and augment our initial perspective. Theory can serve this purpose as well, if we are not overly wedded to a one eye shut model, in which we believe that it is only our own pet theory that has anything of value to offer. I find that using the dual lenses of Bion and Lacan enlarges and enriches my clinical understanding, and helps me to look beyond what either may be saying towards the clinical reality each is pointing to. Each in his own way warns us not to mistake the man for the mission; warns against taking the master as an idol and failing to grapple actively with the ideas being offered. This latter point is crucial in working with those who have been severely waylaid in their life journeys. Failing to attend to the subject who is losing his or her way can make any intervention the wrong thing. Our preliminary and guiding task is always to try to locate the other person, particularly when she cannot find herself. I can recall my own relief as a young adult, looking for answers but merely feeling mis-recognized, at finally being told: "I see that you are here, and you are trying to get there." Being thus located in one's own terms not only provides data that might prove helpful but also usefully affirms that some answers are best found within.

Keeping in mind the importance of the Subject of the inquiry in this way may be Lacan's fundamental offering to the clinician. Felman (1987) notes that at the heart of Lacan is an invitation to recognize our own alienation from ourselves. From this vantage point, we might be able to become more interested in discovering ourselves so that we can better answer questions about the desires that might guide our way if we can recognize them and take them seriously. Lacan invites us to notice how easily and treacherously we can become lost while trying to figure out what is wanted from us such that we neglect the more important task of trying to discover what it is that we, ourselves, actually desire. So, at the core of this volume, you will find Lacan's notion of *the Subject caught by the desire of the Other*. We will use this concept as a checkpoint, a reminder to pause and wonder to what extent we are being true to ourselves, our values, and our understanding of human beings in our work. If we truly believe in a subject-to-subject model of psychotherapy, it is crucial to be able to consider to what extent we are modeling those values or whether we are deferring *our own authority* to some unnamed or unknown Other.

In inviting us to grapple with the *particulars of meaning*, rather than merely conforming to authority, Lacan (1978) encourages a closer reading of Freud than we might have previously achieved. He invites us to move beyond our ideas about the authority of Freud's dictates so that we might experience, alongside Freud, the excitement of the exploration that is the method and process of psychoanalysis. Bion also reads Freud very attentively but offers a closer reading of Freud implicitly rather than explicitly. Taking terms that Freud mentions almost in passing, such as *notation* and *attention,* Bion (1977) defines these terms in relation to the functions they serve in the psychoanalytic process. By highlighting these functions, Bion invites us to pause and to recognize notation as an active aspect of the listening process that marks a node of meaning and helps to focus our attention. Using these terms as the foundation, Bion builds a conceptual map—a *grid*—to assist his efforts toward gaining insight regarding how these experiences mentioned by Freud are ordered and organized in the psychoanalytic process (Charles, 2002a). In creating his grid, Bion not only invites a more measured engagement in the process but also highlights the importance of being able to move beyond the words themselves as we try to discern the purposes for which the words are being used in any particular moment, whether towards development or towards evasion. Bion (like Winnicott) also affirms the importance of *being* and *becoming* as active enterprises so that we can learn from our own experience while also being aware of the many ways in which meanings can be perceived from other perspectives.

For both Bion and Lacan, psychoanalysis aims toward developing our ⟨7 capacity for insight in an active exploration through which obstacles are encountered, recognized, and grappled with. And so, for example, we find Bion (1967a) describing his encounters with a man whose experience could not be symbolized by language in coherent speech but rather could only be inferred over time from whatever inconsistencies and anomalies Bion was able to observe: the *constant conjunctions*—phenomena linked together in patterned ways—that began to emerge over time. Through noticing these patterns, Bion was able to begin to make meaning from the patient's productions and, over time, to give words to his ideas and offer this language back to the patient. In this process, he was able to discern the fundamental hazard of viewing psychosis in terms of a delineation of inevitable otherness. Bion recognized that there are psychotic and non-psychotic elements in each of us, such that we may be communicating at either (or both) levels at any given point in time.

Bion links this observation with Klein's (1930) and Segal's (1957) depictions of the *symbolic equation*, in which a symbol may be felt to *be* something rather than merely representing it. In Lacan's terms, the symbolic equation might be seen as a sign that *marks* meaning rather than as a more complex signifier that is embedded in the consensual system of meanings that he would term Language. Thus, the psychotic confusion between talking about sex versus actually having sex, as though talking about it is the same as performing the act. Take as an example the young woman who, in seeing a nameplate with 'Virginia' written on it, becomes embarrassed, flustered, and confused as to why doctors would put such shocking material on the walls of a hospital. She cannot, in that moment, usefully distinguish between the name Virginia and whatever taboo variant of that name she finds herself faced with.

Using his insights into the particular type of difficulty faced by individuals who cannot tell the difference, for example, between playing the violin in public and masturbating, Bion developed a theory of thinking that focuses on the ability to link thoughts to one another. He saw the psychotic ⟨8 individual as someone who is caught by the need to not think about things that are unacceptable, too painful, or otherwise troublesome, and then is faced with the task of somehow making meaning from unlinked fragments that cannot be linked together. In such a case, meaning literally cannot be made. If we think about what we now know about the fragmented nature of traumatic memory, and about the difficulties in symbolization or mentalization that occur when thoughts are too concrete, we have some notion of how profound were these early insights of Bion. We will consider signifiers and the processes of fragmentation and mentalization more fully in later chapters.

During this same period in which Bion was developing his theories, Lacan (1978, 1993) was developing his own ideas regarding the impasses in which people find themselves, focusing on the developmental task of becoming a Subject in relation to other thinking Subjects. Lacan structures subjective experience according to three dimensions: the Real, which is the experience itself; the Imaginary, which is the personal ideational realm (the realm of thought and fantasy), and the Symbolic, which is the realm of logic, Language, and consensual understanding. For Lacan, we are born into a Real that becomes Imaginary, caught within the confines of our own internal imaginings. Born into the Imaginary of the Other, we enter the world already to some extent invented by our parents, who have invested in us their thoughts, dreams, and desires. The challenge, then, is to begin to come to grips with the ways in which one is caught by the *Desire of the Other*, to come to terms with Limit (we can never be or have everything), and to begin to formulate one's own desires rather than losing oneself in the pursuit of an impossible otherness or a *Jouissance* (limitless pleasure) that is inevitably out of reach.

Although this tension between self and other did not form an explicit part of Bion's work, we find it there implicitly, as he tries to step out from his own shadow to invite us each to learn from our own experience rather than foreclosing the process of discovery by taking false idols and imposing received knowledge without truly encountering the subject of our inquiry. It was for this reason that Bion bristled against the term 'understanding,' which seemed to connote for him the idea that one had reached sufficient familiarity with a subject that one was no longer interested in learning more or exploring other possibilities.

The encounter with the Real or 'O', as Bion puts it, requires a willingness to be present in a given moment. This process of continually trying to encounter ourselves as we are is fundamental to psychoanalytic psychotherapy. For the clinician, this type of deep encounter with another person can be particularly difficult when dealing with psychosis, and also with perversion, in the larger sense in which Lacan used the term. From Lacan's perspective, perversion implies that one derives pleasure from one's symptom such that there is little desire to give it up.

We can have perverse relationships even with our own pain, as we will see in later chapters. Through case vignettes, we will see how eating disorders, borderline phenomena, and even psychosis can become particularly intransigent *because* of the libidinal tie to the symptom. Kleinians (Schafer, 1997) note the aggression and hostility often linked with such attachments that can increase their virulence and persistence, creating the type of perverse relationship with destructive objects or behaviors noted by Lacan. In such instances, the very attempt to overcome the difficulty further entrenches us and keeps us tied to that difficulty. The anorexic, for example, in trying to have no needs, exacerbates her starvation. Her failure to attend to her internal cues of hunger intensifies the distress and therefore also intensifies the strength of the signals marking that distress. The extent of her pain—and, at times, the virulence of her suicidality—paradoxically becomes a sign that she is succeeding. In some ways, the problems persist because they are *mislocated*. Her symptoms locate her problems in relation to food rather than in her inability to develop a self that is sufficiently well grounded to be able to live her life. Her inability to sustain her life, and her inability to directly ask for help, then, successfully mark the fact that she is in trouble. We will consider these dilemmas further in later chapters.

Although, as clinicians, we try to understand our patients and how they have become stuck in their lives, there is also a hazard in imposing our understanding or even in trying too hard to *be helpful*. Winnicott (1971) warns against stealing the patient's creativity by 'knowing too much' and Bion warns against losing sight of ways in which our desire to be good at our jobs can keep patients from discovering whatever they might learn if we can avoid imposing our 'knowledge' on them. Bion (1990) offers a useful metaphor in this regard, suggesting that if we are to understand "the most fundamental and primitive parts of the human mind . . . instead of trying to bring a brilliant, intelligent, knowledgeable light to bear on obscure problems" we should instead "bring to bear a diminution of the 'light'—a penetrating beam of darkness: a reciprocal of the searchlight" (p. 20). Appreciating the possibilities inherent in this darkness can help us tolerate our ignorance rather than immediately trying to overcome it, and to hold steady when we would most like to leap away. Being willing to tolerate moments, hours, days, and weeks of uncertainty and dark despair can be crucial to the ultimate outcome of the treatment. Both Lacan and Bion appreciate that the analyst's desire can be a powerfully obstructive force in the treatment (Bion, 1967b).

This insight also helps to remind us that our work is not amenable to any one-size-fits-all manual that suits all occasions. What may be too much darkness in one moment may be too much light in another. When working with individuals whose affective self-regulation is tenuous, we may find we are expending a great deal of energy trying not to upset the balance, lest we invite further affective storms. At times, all we can really do is recognize explicitly the difficulties encountered by the other person and acknowledge that nothing feels right to them, that talk feels like an attack or an imposition, and silence feels like abandonment. We may not be able to avoid being the bad object, at times, but at least we can recognize our position and commiserate with the poor patient who is stuck sitting with a therapist who is of no value to them whatsoever, at least for the moment.

In the following chapters, we will visit the consulting room, encountering various manifestations of trauma, the ghostly presence that both speaks to us and eludes us, at times through the *empty speech* noted by Lacan, in which the words are devoid of meaning because they are detached from the self; at other times through a perverse invitation to become embroiled in the patient's hopelessness or in our own enjoyment of the psychosis or 'being helpful.' We will encounter the psychotic who speaks unruly truths, who sees too much, hears too much, and does not have sufficient filters to be able to find her own bearings or keep from unsettling those around her. We will encounter the obsessive compulsive who uses routine and ritual as ways of trying to keep from being taken over by the impossible demands of others and becomes psychotic when her refusal fails. We will also encounter the self-object child of the psychotic mother, used and abandoned, who develops the idea that *she* must be an alien but over time begins to recognize and repair her sense of her own humanity. In each of these cases, we will see how the individual gets lost in a subject-to-object relationship and becomes embroiled in trying to undo damage that has already been done in an attempt not to be the object hated by the mother.

In each chapter, we will encounter a clinical concept from the psychoanalytic literature, which we will try to consider from different angles, using the case vignettes to bring those clinical facts to life. When possible, I will present clinical moments rather than offering longer case studies, hoping that in keeping very close to the clinical experience, you will be invited to consider your own experiences in ways that may be most relevant and applicable to your own practice. In trying to show you how I use the concept in my own work, I hope to underscore the central theme guiding this book: that our own personal ethics must be the touchstone guiding our interventions. Given the wealth of available resources, most important is our ability to feel free enough to explore them that we can discover what might be most useful in a given moment. I find that having an array of tools behind me gives me the armament I need when I hit a tough moment. This backing doesn't help me avoid difficult moments, but it affords me a bit more courage, a bit more resilience, and a lot more hope.

Chapter Two

The Subject Caught by the Desire of the Other

In this chapter, we will focus on Lacan's idea of the *Subject caught by the desire of the Other*. In many ways, this book is my response to clinicians who say, "I keep hearing about Lacan but I don't really know anything about his work." Paradoxically, you keep hearing about Lacan because he introduced a way of thinking about clinical work that is fundamentally important *because* it is clinically useful, even though these gems of insight can be difficult to extract from Lacan's dense and often obfuscating language. This denseness, I believe, is partly a function of the territory he is trying to cover but also an attempt to point to the issues without being prescriptive in a way that might encourage us to use the prescriptions rather than entering the territory ourselves. Much like Bion, who encourages us to *learn from our own experience*, for Lacan, the function of psychoanalysis is the development of 26 insight. At the heart of the clinical work is an appreciation of the primary human dilemma of becoming a Subject. It is only by discovering ways in 27 which we come into the world already defined by others' needs and demands that we can then begin to think more explicitly about our own desires and values. As opposed to many theoretical models (including some psychoanalytic ones), where the therapist is seen as the expert who might help the person to change or obtain new knowledge, for Lacan, the therapeutic encounter is an opportunity for the patient to perhaps learn 28 something from his or her own experience. From this perspective, the therapist's job is to pay attention to what the patient is doing with this opportunity, and to track the person as she looks for and hides from whatever she knows or might know about herself. In this chapter, we will look further into this tension, as we consider how we might notice this process and speak to it in the session.

In thinking about the particular focus that Lacan puts on the Subject, note the similarity between Lacan's stance and Bion's focus on learning from experience. Both theorists appreciate the importance of tracking very carefully whatever is happening in the room, and both recognize the fundamental separation between the two people involved. At the core of our work is an encounter between two subjects, each of whom can be destabilized. The therapist's job is to use her own wisdom to try to track what is going on for the patient, and then to try to be useful by either articulating something she has observed or by staying out of the way. This is where we would like to have in mind Winnicott's (1971) adage of not stealing the patient's creativity by *knowing too much* or advertising what we know. At the heart of the matter is the tension between our desire to rely on someone who might Know in some absolute sense, and the price of this reliance in preventing us from learning whatever we might discover if we were to rely more heavily on—and thereby build—our own resources.

Imagine, if you will, sitting with a patient who is feeling hopeless and seems intent on wanting to die. This is scary stuff. Part of us responds empathically—but also selfishly—wanting to counter the despair and sense of inevitability. This is an important moment of choice. When we feel something in us rising in opposition to something in the patient, it is useful to sit with this desire and to think about it rather than to act on it immediately. Thinking about our own internal tension in relation to the tension that the patient must be experiencing helps us to situate the dilemma where it belongs: in the person who has hired us to focus on him.

As Kleinians note, our feelings in the session—our countertransference—can be our best guide to affective tensions in the analytic field. Being able to think about to what extent our internal sensations may be in empathic alignment with or complementary to the patient's own experience can be an important tool (Racker, 1968; Joseph, 1985). The feeling that the patient is splitting off one part of his ambivalence so that it only registers in us and not in him is what Object Relations theorists talk about in terms of *projective identification*, a useful way of indexing this clinical fact. From a Lacanian perspective, however, one might conceptualize this dilemma a bit differently, in terms of the *Subject caught by the desire of the Other*. From this perspective, we are all born into a world in which we have already been formulated as a subject. Our parents' fantasies and fears provide opportunities and stumbling blocks that help to shape us as individuals. At various points, we rebel against these constraints and begin to develop our own perspective, our own voice. Our subjectivity, however, is always embedded in the world as we have experienced it, which initially seems to be just *the way things are*. Breaking into that presumption affords the possibility of choice and of change.

Lacan viewed psychoanalysis as an ethical imperative, in which there is clearly something fundamental at stake: the individual's relationship to him or herself as the subject of the conversation. If we take the problem of one's own subjectivity in relation to others as the fundamental dilemma at the core of any treatment, then our work is guided by that rubric. What follows is that any attempt to defer to the other as Expert or Solver of Problems further complicates the core problem. It is important, then, for the therapist to track this tendency to defer to the other (in herself as well as in the patient). From this perspective, we can wonder about the person's desires that have been hidden behind his ideas about what might or might not be valued or desired by the other.

To be faced with dire problems is also disregulating for the therapist, bringing our own self-righting mechanisms into play. It is easy at such moments to look for an external Authority—some rule we might follow to reassure ourselves when we feel we have lost our way. The most valuable tools that the psychodynamic clinician has at her disposal, in such moments, are her ideas about unconscious processes. These ideas help her to organize an understanding of the conflicting feelings within her, as she also thinks about her own experiences studying those internal feelings. Let me give you a few examples to help clarify this issue, and to highlight ways in which these tensions may be at the heart of many of our clinical dilemmas.

Working with people who are in dire straits is distressing and a part of us yearns to reduce the distress through action. I have learned to notice my own sense of urgency as a cue that invites me to sit back and think about what is going on. My more reflective mind knows that "solving a problem" or being in opposition to a patient is not necessarily conducive to constructive work, but it wasn't until I encountered Lacan that I had a more extensive way of thinking about the core dilemma at the heart of this tension. Previously, my main entry point into this dilemma had been through Bion's grid (1977/1989), through which he invites us to look beyond the content to try to track the process.

Bion devised his grid as a way of trying to index the underlying processes at play in the psychoanalytic encounter. He uses this grid as a two-dimensional map, tracking on one axis the *complexity* of the thought, from intuition or metaphor towards further refinement and abstraction. On the other axis, he tracks the *uses* to which the statement is being put, whether to define an experience, to defend against defining it (lying), or to probe or further illuminate material that is becoming clearer. In this way, Bion tries to track the complexity of thinking and also the use to which the thought is being applied (Charles, 2002a). So, for example, a statement can be used simply to define or index facts; it can be a negation; a false statement used for defensive purposes; a realization; a theory; a probe for further information, and so on. The grid, then, as a way of indexing the types of functions that statements might have, helps us to think about what the patient might be doing when he utters a given phrase. "I don't know," for example, can be a statement of fact, a defensive maneuver, or an outright lie. Bion's grid reminds us that any given statement might serve a myriad of functions, and that we should be listening intently and openly in order to be in a position to "get" whatever is being said, or to check in with the patient when we are not sure.

"Getting the message" can at times be quite complicated; a person can say and unsay something at the same time. Think, for example, of the child who says: "stop yelling at me" when no voice has been raised. The parent can then say: "I wasn't yelling at you," which would be both true and untrue. The untrue portion would be to fail to acknowledge the critical tone, which the child had indexed as "being yelled at." The parent who can notice both aspects helps the child to make sense of an interpersonal world in which more than one message can be delivered simultaneously. That child is then freer to notice and make sense of subtleties of meaning when they are communicated in daily interactions. When such ambiguity is denied, however, it is easy for the child to become caught in a struggle to obtain acknowledgment, resulting in the type of either/or battle that is all too familiar to us as therapists, the kind of double-bind pointed to in the literature as a major cause of severe mental illness.

Finding oneself in such a battle is a very good clue that there is a false dichotomy being played out that should be attended to as such. One way out of such a dilemma is to note it explicitly: "It seems as though we are each taking one side of a question as though only one side might be true without having to take into account the other." Or "It seems as though you are so focused on the part of you that wants to die that I wind up being the voice of the part of you that wants to live, as though that was not also a part of you that I am registering and speaking for." One might then go further and say something about the danger of being caught in that way: that if the person can really deny the part of himself that wants to live, it will be even harder to find a viable way to build a life. Notice that in those suggested statements the focus is on the person in relation to himself, bringing us back to Lacan.

Psychoanalytic ideas teach us to resonate to the multiple layers of meaning that can be present in any given interchange. Jim Grotstein (2009a, b) very explicitly highlights this way of listening by titling his recent volumes on Kleinian/Bionian technique: *But at the Same Time and on Another Level.* Lacan also points to the multiple layers of meaning when he writes that "the unconscious is structured like a language." This structural relationship between words and meaning also structures our relationship with ourselves. For example, whatever is deemed to be an unacceptable character trait will either be very difficult for me to notice in myself, or will be so salient that I stumble over it. By highlighting the relationship of words to meaning, Lacan invites us to consider more carefully presumptions we make that can cover over the very information we are seeking. Alerted to this gap, we are in a better position to consider ways in which an individual becomes captured by such meanings within the context of his relationship to himself and others. At the core of the dilemma is the capacity to think of oneself as a separate person in relation to others rather than to defer one's needs or desires without even quite noticing that they are being deferred.

The attachment literature has highlighted how self and meaning are constructed in the context of social relationships. Stern (1985) describes the complicated transitions occurring over time through which the subject emerges, marking the importance of relationships in successfully negotiating developmental milestones. In his papers about transitional objects and the use of an object, Winnicott (1971) points to essential transitions that are also relevant to the relationship between patient and therapist. These papers delineate some of the complexities involved as we grapple with our dependence and learn to become separate subjects in relation to others who are also separate subjects. Tracking this transition, as Winnicott describes it, we see the child encountering his need—or, in Lacan's terms, his desire—and the limits of his ability to address this need. Initially, the baby's needs and desires are inextricably tied to the parent and to her ability to fulfill them. In the presence of a *good enough mother*, the child learns to tolerate distress and to satisfy his desires over time, whether by discovering soothing objects that are under his control or by learning that his rage does not kill off the other (Winnicott, 1971). Internalizing affective self-regulation depends on our ability to construct meanings such that separation and distance can be tolerated and managed.

In the consulting room, the clinician is in a position to notice failures in this developmental progression. If we are attuned to this dilemma, deficits in affective self-regulation can be seen at the core of the patient's distress. These deficits are inevitably embedded in a story that tells how that individual has been caught by the needs and desires of the parents in ways that are largely invisible. This is where learning the history can be fundamentally important, so that we can see more clearly how relationships are configured in that individual's universe. Our interest in the tangle helps the person to notice for herself some of those tangles, helping to distinguish between *the way things are,* in an inevitable sense, from the way things have become. I find that it is easy, as a therapist, to feel that my job is to maneuver my way out of a difficult situation rather than to recognize the impasse. This is another important choice point to be able to recognize: when we feel as though we should be "fixing something" rather than discussing it. In those moments, when our own internal affective disregulation invites us into action, it is important to be able to hold steady and reflect on the layers of meanings rather than jump to the surface to "fix" the problem.

As an example, let's think about the patient who accuses us, in whatever fashion, of being a "bad therapist." There is the implicit or explicit accusation that, if we were just doing a better job, she would be feeling better or managing better. Whereas it is important for the therapist to be able to feel implicated in this problem—we have, indeed, not managed to help the person out of her dilemma—it is also important to decide whether or not we believe that this is, should be, or even can be our job. If we think of our job as providing people with opportunities to obtain greater insight into their problems so that they might be able to come up with more adaptive solutions to their problems—or at least more clearly choose not to—then we find ourselves in the role of companion on a journey rather than pilot of the boat. From this perspective, I can call out navigational signs I notice along the way, in hope that these signs will be useful to the pilot. I can also make observations about difficulties in communicating, so that if my attempts to provide useful information are not useful, or are dysregulating, I can pause to try to understand that particular impasse. I like to be as clear as I can with people about how I see my role, so that they can perhaps understand how I am positioning myself and so that if they are looking for a pilot they can go try to find one.

To illustrate, here is a moment from my work with "Alice," a young woman whose history had left her able to perform very well academically and in work situations, but without a clear or reliable sense of self. One of her struggles had been with food (see Charles, 2006a, 2007, for a fuller elaboration of this case), and we came to a point where she steadfastly insisted that she could not eat. This was a point she had come to repeatedly in past treatments and the result had invariably been hospitalization, stabilization of weight, and then a return to the habits that would eventually bring her back to this dire point. As a therapist, I was in a quandary. I knew that what she was saying was both true and not true. Certainly, she did know how to eat and was capable of eating—in the abstract sense—but just as certainly she had come to a point where she was not capable of making choices that would result in bringing food into her body. I had wished that I could help her to find a way to bring herself to eat but had not been able to do so.

One of the difficulties I faced in my work with Alice was that she would often "speak" silently, through facial gesture or mute despair. Her relative absence left me trying to translate these communications into words. Although, for me, these attempts were hypotheses (Bion's *definitory statements*), Alice tended to receive my conjectures as facts or demands. It was at times virtually impossible to position myself as a separate subject in relation to Alice. Her facility in slipping to the side in our conversations gave me information regarding where she did locate herself as a subject, and provided more evidence to my internal conjectures that it was in that very slipping to the side that her aggression (and therefore also an important part of her subjectivity) was located.

This was a case in which there were continuing assaults on the frame from the very beginning, bringing up questions regarding what can legitimately be expected from a therapist and from a patient. What are the limits in what two individuals can do together, and what does it mean to come up against such limits? With individuals in dire circumstances, we are up against very complicated clinical questions regarding how we might acknowledge the extent of the distress without perpetuating what might become a deadly enactment. The anorexic brings us into this arena by enacting the dilemma with which she has been faced regarding how she might survive with insufficient sustenance. Inevitably, the therapist finds herself cast as the insufficient savior in this enactment. Managing to accept the inevitability of failure—that we cannot truly save another person from him or herself—is an essential precondition for considering how the person might come to save herself.

Much as Alice has felt constricted by the Other, my experience is of alternatively being held captive by her deadliness or of having the roles suddenly shift so that I become the Persecutor in the drama. I am expecting too much and giving too little; she is wounded by my lack of care. In this way, we reach another critical juncture where my empathic concern can be triggered and I might try to repair a wrong that cannot usefully be repaired. If, alternatively, I can hold steady and reflect on the dilemma, I might be able to say something to Alice that might help her to think about it. Enactments are not necessarily avoidable and at times may be the patient's only way of communicating facts that cannot yet be put into words. Often, it is by finding ourselves in the midst of an enactment that we begin to better understand the problem.

So, for example, Alice tells me that she cannot eat. I have the sense that this is both true and untrue: that she is unable to find her way into eating once again. I ask if it would help her to be able to eat with me. She says that it might. Once, again, I feel myself in a treacherous position, where I could easily try to push her into eating or insist that she eat. If I do that, however, there is no way for her to choose to eat. I feel I am at the edge of a precipice where a great deal is at stake. On one side, we fall into a game where I am keeping her alive in spite of herself. On the other side is the possibility that she might get some traction in this business of being able to take in sufficient nourishment such that she might be able to sustain her own life. I tell her that she needs to decide how to proceed. We can try to figure out together if she can use me as a way of beginning to structure eating for herself. We arrange for her to come for breakfast the next day. I have food ready, and we sit with the food.

It is odd to be sitting and eating together, knowing that what she has told me is both true and untrue. I believe, however, that there is some potential value for Alice in my recognition that it is not the feeding that is important but rather her ability to feed herself. She talks about her internal struggles over eating in ways that show me that she is trying to take responsibility for taking care of her own needs. "I was thinking about not coming in," she says. "I watched myself trying to find a way out, watched myself lying to myself about it, and wasn't sure what I would do. I thought that I should be able to do it myself, but I realized that I wouldn't, and so I came." In this statement, we can see Alice's reflective function coming forward as she owns and tries to come to grips with her own ambivalence. In this way, she comes forward as the Subject in her own life, an individual who could not manage to find a way to eat, but then, with my assistance, finds her way back into eating. At that point, she could no longer say that she could not eat without also recognizing that she had, within herself, a means for beginning to move from not-eating to eating.

From that time forward, when Alice would say that she was not able to eat, it was no longer a demand for someone else to take over but rather a definitory statement about a familiar impasse in which she found herself embroiled. From that perspective, we could think and talk together about the meanings of this not-eating for Alice, and she could continue to reflect on the ambivalent feelings that come forward in this particular way for her. The demand to "save me from myself" is a complicated invitation. There is a huge price to pay when joining someone who truly believes that she does not have the wherewithal to save herself. I try, in such a moment, to hold steady and to leave a space to discuss with the person what choices might be available if she truly does not feel that she can keep herself safe. Behaving as though she cannot make an affirmative move towards safeguarding her own life is itself a major statement, one that should be articulated if at all possible. Articulating the dilemma before taking action marks the possibility of choice such that we can then discuss various resolutions, understanding that each has costs and benefits.

Chapter Three

Stumbling over the Gap

"The Unconscious Is Structured Like a Language"

In this chapter, we will focus on Lacan's (1977a, 1978a) ideas about the Unconscious, structure, language, and the gap. These concepts help us to take more seriously what we stumble over in our work with individuals who cannot necessarily tell us directly where the trouble lies but who show us the trouble over time. As noted in the last chapter, Lacan (1978b, c) says that the Unconscious is structured like a language, in this way inviting us to recognize relationships between meanings, much as Bion (1977) describes relationships between psychoanalytic elements. As Freud notes and memory research affirms, relationships in the unconscious are more fluid and less clearly differentiated than in conscious, rational thought. If we are to work effectively as psychodynamic therapists, we need to be conversant in both the rational language of secondary process and the unconscious logic of primary process. One of Freud's gifts was to focus our attention on the many ways in which the unconscious inserts itself into our daily lives and thereby invites recognition of layers of meaning that might otherwise go unattended. Thinking of the unconscious as structured like a language invites us to observe the logic of the unconscious and to notice the places where there are gaps or disjunctions. Recognizing the inevitability of gaps also helps us to tolerate limits we come to in our work. We will look further into this issue in a later chapter, where we will discuss Lacan's ideas about empty speech and Bion's ideas about attacks on linking, but for now I would like to address more specifically this issue of stumbling over a gap or disjunction that can alert us to the presence (or absence) of a fact not yet clearly articulated.

19

4o

The concept of the gap seems crucial to an understanding of Lacan, because it is the gap that also points to his ideas about Lack. For Lacan, the fundamental human dilemma circles around Lack. Although at some level we know that we can't be or have everything, we still encounter this reality with some resistance. We know that we can't be both male and female, and yet we are reluctant to relinquish the hope of "having it all." The fantasy of being both must be given up in order to figure out what kind of male or female we are going to be. We initially do have the idea that someone might have it all. Our parents seem confident and capable, as though they must have all the answers. Of course, none of us can ever have all the answers, but the idea that we are supposed to be more than we are can be both compelling and destabilizing. Certainly, as therapists, we stumble over that idea all the time. The patient is talking and I think I am following and then, all of a sudden, she stops and seems to be waiting for something. Did I miss something, I wonder? Part of me feels uncomfortable, as though I have committed some sort of gaffe, and I want to cover it over, fill up the empty space, pretend I didn't miss whatever I believe I missed.

This is an important choice point in the treatment. Sometimes I succumb to my anxiety and pretend, hoping I will "catch up" and not really have missed anything. Through this pretense, I miss the opportunity to inquire into the gap and perhaps discover something important about whatever occurred during that moment of disjunction. Even though I invite the patient to say everything that comes to mind and to skip nothing—and I have the idea that it is precisely those things he desires to skip over that are most important to say—I can still behave as though the pretense of knowing is more important than actually trying to come to grips with whatever material actually manifests itself in the session.

At other times, however, I can override my discomfort and am able to meet the challenge. I can ask: did I miss something? I can note that there has been a gap and ask about the patient's experience of it; whether he stumbled over something and, if so, what he knows about it. If I can do that, I might discover that the stumbling had nothing directly to do with my actions or inactions. I might also discover that the stumbling did have something directly or indirectly to do with me. I might suspect that even though the patient does not consciously know it—or perhaps merely is not saying it— that he likely stumbled over a gap in my attention that he did, indeed, sense. Once again, if I can keep my mind in the moment, I can wonder with the patient about why we stumbled at that particular moment. Is there something hard to notice or come to grips with that we are both avoiding? Being interested in the gap potentially opens up the possibility of greater insight, whereas avoiding the subject closes down that possibility. This is the choice point between growth or evasion that Bion (1977) pinpoints as the critical challenge in any moment of discomfort.

This type of clinical moment came to the fore relatively early in my professional development when I was working with a man for whom "what was missing" was an important factor that he stumbled over recurrently (see Charles, 1998 for a fuller explication). "Aron" had been born with birth defects that affected not only his personal appearance but also his ability to perform various functions. His parents insisted that he behave as though there were no deficit and so he learned, rather than feeling proud of what he was able to accomplish in spite of the disability, to be ashamed whenever the disability could be recognized. Any failure, then, was a dual failure: there was the overt task that had not been accomplished, but there was also the more insidious failure to sustain the very illusion that was also a fundamental denial of himself as the unique individual he was.

I found working with Aron arduous because of this quality of illusion that had the effect of making me feel very dull and unable to sustain attention in our sessions. As I tried to make sense of my own lifelessness and lack of vitality in my sessions with Aron, I found valuable Winnicott's (1971) distinction between fantasying, characterized as an empty avoidance of reality, versus playing, which affords sufficient space between self and other to be able to engage with a fact or a person creatively. In this sense, fantasying can be seen as a repetitive thread that precludes creative engagement or working through. I was experiencing the lack of space almost literally, as a lack of air that precluded not only engagement but also my very aliveness. In Lacan's terms, the fantasying covers over a gap, thereby making it even more difficult to grapple with whatever problems are underlying.

When the therapist's curiosity is sufficiently thwarted, it is as though 41 there is no air in the room. As our interest is dampened, so is our vitality. With Aron, for example, I am struck by the omission of any reference to his physical deformities, and I wonder how those deformities affected him as he was growing up. When I inquire, however, into this gap in his narrative, he informs me with some derision that most people do not notice the deformities. As he says this, the implication seems to be that most people have the courtesy not to ask such questions because they are polite enough to pretend not to notice something that is best left hiding in plain sight. I feel chastised, and assume that most people would drop the subject there. We are not, however, engaged in a "normal" relationship and so I persist. He is initially dysregulated and angry at my insistence on breaking through this barrier he has set. Shaming me for my interest is initially effective in inhibiting it. As I persist, however, over time my interest in his experience helps him to become interested in material that had been inaccessible because of the ways in which his inhibition had sealed over this topic, foreclosing conversation.

In Aron's family, being a success had meant behaving as though there were no deformity and no handicap. If the handicap became apparent, Aron had failed. Thus, he was not only ashamed of the handicap itself, which likely invited stares or avoidance of gaze, particularly when he was young, but he also learned to be ashamed of his inability to successfully hide signs of his handicap and, with it, his individuality. This tension—between facts that he could not erase or entirely overcome, and a desire to be a subject who could be valued—seemed impossible to resolve without denying himself in the process. For me, the tension was experienced as discomfort and boredom. I would begin each session with renewed determination to follow his speech but inevitably find myself lost. Initially, I tried to overcome the gap by "catching up," hoping that I might re-find the thread sufficiently to be able to play my part in the interaction. Over time, however, I became more interested in what we might be playing out in this way, and wondered more explicitly about why there were these repeated gaps in our work together.

Even though I know at an intellectual level how important it is to inquire into the gaps, it can be an extremely difficult goal to accomplish in any given moment. As mentioned previously, shame was an important part of this dynamic. Along with the shame that Aron induced as a means for avoiding painful topics, was the further difficulty, for me, of the shame attached to being caught in a moment of not-knowing. Shame can be particularly lethal because, experientially, it has such a compelling truth value that it can be hard to believe the story we are telling ourselves as we try to address or relieve the shame. This disjunction between what we might know in our conscious mind if we weren't so flooded with emotion, and what we feel to be true in a moment of intense emotion, is a useful distinction to have in mind when our patients are stuck in such a bind. At those moments, telling the patient anything can feel insulting and attacking because the virulence of the emotion makes it difficult to access reflective functions. In such moments, it is important to have in mind lessons from the attachment literature that highlight the prosodies of affective engagement. When affects are running high, it is important to be able to meet the affect of the patient with resonant empathy before trying to encourage a shift.

The literature on early attachment shows the power of nonverbal communication, through which we can meet someone in a difficult moment by responding with tone, facial movement, or bodily gesture in a way that mirrors the affect of the other person. This type of empathic responsiveness tends to produce a feeling of "being understood," which for most people is inherently soothing. For some individuals, however, attachment has been so dangerous that closeness can signal danger. There really are no absolute rules in this work that can be applied without considering the individual's responsiveness. As a result, our attunement to our patients offers our best guide as to what constitutes soothing for that individual. With sufficient moment by moment attention, our efforts to accommodate to the needs of the other can help them to calm down, enhancing the ability to make a shift in thinking or feeling.

So, for example, I am sitting with a patient who is experiencing shame at her inability to be more effective in her relationships. With what seems to be all good intentions, I tell her that she shouldn't feel so badly. She feels hurt and attacked as though being told that she is managing badly. My instinctual reaction is to argue with her, to say that she is misunderstanding me, thus putting myself into the position of expert—the One who Knows. In this move, I lose sight of her as the Subject and then cannot see how I am, indeed, telling her that she is wrong and I am right. If I can regain my bearings, I might be able to recognize my mistake and acknowledge it, going back to the impasse, trying to track where I went astray, and thinking about what I might usefully say at that point. I might merely affirm that I could understand why she would be angry with me for failing to recognize the difficulty she was describing. I might also say something about the interaction between the two of us. Perhaps most crucial, however, is to recognize the point of impasse: the moment when she was trying to say something about her experience and I had run over her in my eagerness to "be helpful" or to "fix something" rather than maintaining my subordinate role in relation to her own self-discovery.

When we are working with individuals whose development has been impeded by trauma, it is particularly important to be able to track the moment by moment interactions in sessions. Trauma interferes with self-regulatory processes, making it difficult for us to keep our bearings much less to be able to think about what has happened or how we would like to proceed. Many of us become psychotherapists because we would like to be helpful to others. While this may be a laudable goal in the abstract, the desire to be helpful can be problematic in practice, particularly when we are sitting with someone who is in deep trouble not easily attenuated. Sitting with someone in dire distress is dysregulating, and it may be difficult at times to know whether our desire is to fix the other person's distress or our own.

At such points of tension, it is very important to be able to reach an agreement with the other person regarding what we are, indeed, doing together. If we have a fantasy that we can truly relieve the other person's distress, then we may be signing on for an absolutely impossible task. We cannot, in the final analysis, truly solve another person's problems. We may be able to offer useful insights but it is really up to them what they do with what we offer. Failing to recognize the limits of what we can and cannot do for another person invites us into an impossible place where we will inevitably fail. This failure also misdirects our efforts away from the more pressing question regarding how the patient's ambivalence might be recognized and worked with so that he can find ways to move beyond his own impasse.

One of the places where we can find ourselves in this type of impossible circle is with suicidal patients. When a person comes in and tells us how much they want to die and how impossible living has become, one empathic response is to resist the idea that death is inevitable. The emotional tension in the room can be so highly charged that we might lose our bearings and try to do something about the problem rather than talking with the patient about his experience. Although at some level we know that this person has come to us, in part, because she is hoping to find a way out of wanting to die, our anxiety may be raised to the point where it is difficult to do whatever work might be required. This tension deserves our attention. If I am too worried about whether or not the patient will be alive from session to session, I am not likely to be able to be terribly useful. Although I can't control what she does or does not do outside of sessions, I do want to feel that we have a working agreement that will enable us to work through what promises to be a difficult period for us both.

One factor that can make it difficult to reach such a working agreement can be our own ambivalence regarding having limits. It is easy to have the fantasy that other therapists may have patients who successfully complete suicide but that we ourselves are somehow immune. This fantasy even makes it difficult to read an account of a completed suicide with any real empathy. At some level, we are distancing ourselves from the account; believing that we, of course, would have done things differently. This would not, could not happen to us. That distancing, then, puts us in danger of failing to recognize that no one is necessarily immune from such a terrible possibility.

Suicide may be the most extreme example of how we can come up against the fact of our own limits. This fact is not only an insult to our narcissism, but also raises very real fears about what it means to have limits when so much is at stake. This is a factor we all struggle with whenever a patient successfully kills him or herself, no matter whose patient it is. If we are honest with ourselves, and don't react disjunctively by comforting ourselves with the idea that this can only happen to those unnamed others who are, perhaps, less capable, less sensitive, less something—if we are honest with ourselves, we know that, but for the grace of God, fate, or destiny, there go I.

At some point we have to come up against these difficult possibilities and really try to grapple with what it means to play such an important part in other people's lives and yet have very real and absolute limits to our power or ability to control the events in other people's lives. We all come up against this issue of limits in our practice, and yet it can feel as though the limit marks some deficit in ourselves, rather than a fact we must learn to contend with. Note how this idea can be particularly dangerous when we identify with the part of our patient that feels as though her struggles mark her as deficient. Once again, we see how virulent an emotion shame can be, inviting us to avoid addressing problems rather than confronting them directly. This hazard makes it particularly important for us as clinicians to speak honestly about our experiences so that we can help one another to find our own way as best we can. Honest conversation about the terrible difficulties we face in relation to the limits we come to in our work can help us reflect more deeply about what happens when we come up hard against our fears. These types of honest conversations amongst colleagues help to support us and help us to feel less alone and therefore a bit less anxious in times of strain.

I came up against this issue quite early in my career in two different ways. I am hoping that offering two very different stories might help us to locate ourselves within some of the complexities we encounter when we come up against the issue of suicide and, with it, the inevitability of encountering Limit. Suicide is not a subject where we can have definitive answers that will inevitably keep us safe. So, then, it becomes important to be able to think about what happens when we come up against our limits; what happens when we come up against our fears.

Whatever structures we might be able to put into place to support ourselves and to help us keep our bearings, when the issue of suicide enters the room, it is a force to be reckoned with. How we reckon with it can be crucially important to the life of the patient, to our lives, and to the life of the treatment. Unfortunately, as I hope you will see from my examples, there are no easy or clear solutions to these dilemmas, particularly as the resolution of one can put at risk the other.

The first event occurred while I was still in training, under the ostensibly safe rubric of the training clinic. I was working with a young man who was classically bipolar, with all the attendant brilliance and grandiosity and disdain one infers from this diagnosis. In the transference, it was never quite clear whether I actually had anything to offer him. It was clear, however, that he would be the one to make this type of judgment. He set the standards. The only question was whether I might come up to them.

When the issue of suicide entered the consulting room, I was in a predicament. He tossed his suicidality at me as his parting shot when leaving the room, giving us no time to explore his feelings or needs in the session. My sense was that he was using this issue as a marker for the extent of his distress, and also as a way to torment me. He had already made it clear that the frame was an essential component of our ability to work together, including his injunction that no telephone calls be made between sessions. Breaking the frame would break the treatment. So, then, how do I deal with a threat that he extends at the end of a session? Do I contain the work within the bounds of the treatment frame, or do I move outside?

My sense was that the treatment depended on my ability to contain my own distress that had been evoked (quite intentionally, I believed) by this parting shot of his. He needed me to be able to contain my anxiety about his suicidal feelings and to thus keep his suicidality in the realm of feelings to be talked about rather than behaviors to be managed. However, I was not entirely on my own. I was working within the parameters of a treatment clinic, where I was offered some safety from responsibility but in return gave up some measure of control. I sought the advice of the clinic director, knowing, in some sense, that by aligning with the structure of the clinic, I was sacrificing the life of the treatment. I don't know how I could have done otherwise. It was not solely my choice to make, because the consequences would affect others.

I made my move with a heavy heart, as it did, indeed, configure the ending of the treatment. My patient was enraged not only at my calling him between sessions but also by my insistence that we come up with a plan that would keep him safe. My inability to keep the frame my patient needed—by keeping the threat of the suicide within the bounds of feelings expressed, rather than pragmatic realities invoked—killed the treatment. Knowing what I know now, particularly from my reading of Lacan, I can see how helpful it might have been to have laid out the dilemma to my patient, to have made the predicament—as he was creating it—explicit and visible. Then, whether or not the treatment continued, he would have been left with a statement about how his defenses protect him but also leave him stuck.

At the other end of the continuum is an experience that occurred a few years later, when I was an intern. I was still bounded by the fact that I was working within an organization but this was a more loosely configured system. I also had more internal authority due to my previous experiences and by virtue of my role, which was configured more as a professional than as a student.

I had been working for some time with a young woman who had a great deal of potential but was extremely fragile. She experienced recurrent bouts of despair so severe that she had hospitalized herself repeatedly as a way of keeping herself safe. Unfortunately, these safety precautions had also taken their toll. Her incursions into the inpatient mental health system had violated her in profound ways. On one particular occasion that I remember vividly, I could barely recognize the individual who emerged from the institution. She seemed like a "bag-lady," empty, having lost herself in the process of seeking assistance for her despair.

As this young woman began to develop more of a sense of self, she faced a quandary: how could she survive her most dire periods without exacerbating them by going back to the hospital? Throughout this period of time, her safety was exceptionally important to me. I felt, to a large extent, responsible for it. It would have been helpful to have been able to talk directly about this dilemma, in which her safety seemed handed to me in an impossible manner. This abdication of agency made it difficult for her to take on the protective functions she needed to put into play. I did not as yet, however, have the conceptual tools or the language with which to have effectively explored these issues with her. I only knew I felt responsible for something I was not at all sure I could manage. Even though I could recognize ways in which important figures in her life would become caught in this very dynamic, I was not able to shift away from the sense of emergency sufficiently to be able to engage in a more reflective discussion of the dynamics at play.

During one of these phases of escalating tension, we reached a crisis point. We discussed the feelings pressing on her and we tried to understand why these pressures were coming to the fore so intensively at this particular point in time. We worked hard. We enlarged our understanding and yet, when the time came to end the session, I had no assurance that the immediate threat had been relieved sufficiently that I would ever see her again. I can still remember how dire were my feelings of fear and sadness. I also recall the heaviness of my feelings of resignation as I said goodbye to this woman, not knowing if I would ever see her again. At that moment, it was quite clear to me that the decision to continue the struggle or to end it was not in my hands. That moment represented a fundamental and pivotal shift in my position as a therapist. I had come to the limits of what I could and could not do and was both humbled and set free.

I was fortunate. This woman told me later that my hope, my faith, and my investment in her had helped carry her through those dark hours. And so, I knew that I had been able to accomplish at least that much. I can also think in retrospect about how I might have managed the work more competently. But I also see how the attempt to look backward, to revise and repair, is a potential trap if it leaves us with the illusion that if we just do it right, everything will be fine. I also know that the ultimate decision to live or to die is not in our hands. It therefore matters very much how the patient sees it. Now, when I work with someone who expresses suicidal thoughts or feelings, I try very actively to understand the meanings of these thoughts and feelings so that we can reach an understanding together that helps to attenuate the distress. I also try to distinguish between the wish to die as an expression of intense feelings versus the intent to die in terms of behavior that must be managed.

We need to be able to consider to what extent talk of suicide represents a communication of the extent of the person's pain that we must be able to tolerate in order to work it through or, alternatively, a statement that the person does not feel safe and needs some active problem-solving regarding how to deal with safety issues. Talk of suicide can also represent a sadomasochistic enactment, in which the therapist can feel held hostage by the patient who acts out her hostility by attacking the therapist with this very dire material and all it represents. In working with suicidal individuals, I have found it very important to be clear in my own mind about the limits of what I can and cannot do, and also what I am and am not willing or able to take on at any given point in time.

If a person really wants to kill himself, he can find a way to do it. My presumption, then, is that if he is working with me, he is at least ambivalent about dying. If I am worried about a patient's safety, I try to be explicit about this working idea I have, as a way of checking things out to see where we are with one another. I try to be very clear that I can't be in charge of saving her, but I am willing to work with her while she figures out how to save herself. If we are going to work with suicidal or self-harming patients, it is important to be able to recognize the perverse relationship with pain that develops when pain is linked to "home" (Novick & Novick, 1996). We will discuss perversion and sadomasochistic relationships with pain in Chapter 5.

For now, however, in keeping with the current chapter's theme of stumbling, let's end by highlighting the importance of being able to stumble over the real limits we come to in a given moment with a patient. It is during such moments of high affective arousal that we most need to be able to hold steady. Maintaining or regaining our reflective functions in such moments helps us to consider the impasse and to think about how best to proceed, always accepting that we are human and have limits as to what we can and cannot do. Part of our job is to recognize those limits and to try to help the patient find further or other assistance if that seems needed. When working with individuals who become so severely dysregulated that they at times find it difficult to bear the pain or even think about how to manage in a given moment, one of the limits we come to is the dysregulation itself. We will turn to a consideration of the disruptive and dysregulating effects of shame in Chapter 4 and will then consider dysregulation in relation to mentalization and psychosocial development.

Chapter Four

Shame and the Possibility of Insight

In this chapter we will consider the inverse relationship between shame and the possibility of insight. Affect theorist Sylvan Tomkins notes that the hallmark of shame is the aversion of gaze. Part of this reaction is an inability to confront one's self as represented by the other's gaze. In Winnicott's "good enough relationship," the parent eases dysregulation sufficiently that 50 the child can once again encounter the parent's loving gaze. Lodged once again securely in a world in which one feels one has value, the child can continue to learn. If, however, the other's gaze has been unduly critical, one feels as though one is lacking. From this position, it can be difficult to meet the other's gaze, which can result in ongoing cycles of isolation, shame, and despair. Lacan positions the psychoanalytic encounter, not in terms of a possibility of "cure" but rather as an opportunity through which one might obtain insight. This learning, according to Bion (1977) is predicated upon one's ability to sustain interest rather than turning away. Shame, however, entails a rupture of interest. If we see shame as a fundamental stumbling 51 point that can keep important information unknowable, then we might be able to consider the person's predicament as he approaches his shame in our presence. Crucial to the clinician's task is the ability to track the other person's encounter with his own inhibitions, including shame, so that we can help him to notice and empathically connect with his own resistance. Considering a few clinical moments will help us to explore this dilemma. In the following chapters, we will consider a variety of the clinical difficulties we encounter with individuals for whom shame disrupts the ability to relate positively to self and other.

Foremost in the writings of Lacan and Bion is the dilemma of the subject in relation to himself. For each, real learning can only occur if it is experience-near. Such learning requires the ability to take oneself sufficiently seriously, a capacity that is fundamentally impeded by shame. Experientially, shame breaks the interpersonal bond and leaves us feeling alone and lacking. In this way, it is perhaps the most isolating and most devastating of affects because it tends to invite pseudo-solutions that further alienate us from ourselves. It is as though we would need to deny the shame in order to repair the rupture but denying the shame means denying a part of ourselves. These pseudo-resolutions have been marked in the psychoanalytic literature by terms such as the type of "false self" organization that Winnicott (1965) suggests can be a defense against psychotic anxiety. Winnicott describes the development of the false self in relation to the mother's failure to recognize the baby's gesture, rather substituting her own in its place. This dilemma is also marked by Lacan in his descriptions of the Subject caught by the desire of the Other. Our failure to obtain recognition from important others is the type of rupture that affect theorist Sylvan Tomkins (1963) depicts in his descriptions of the physiological experience of shame.

Anticipating an understanding of human behavior, memory, and cognition that would increasingly recognize the pivotal role of affect, Tomkins (1962, 1963) developed a theory that describes how our motivations, values, and actions are fundamentally organized and circumscribed by affect. Tomkins's theory highlights the experiential aspects of emotion, noting the universal behavior patterns that are seen across cultures. We recognize affects both in terms of our own physiological experience and also in what we read in the faces of others. For Tomkins, shame replaces Freud's drives as the potentiating factor that can increase or inhibit any other emotion or motivation. He describes shame in terms of a disruption of interest or pleasure that is recognized most fundamentally by the aversion of gaze. The sudden rupture breaks the interpersonal bond, leaving the individual feeling alone and alienated. Tomkins (1963) describes how profoundly shame can interfere with the ability to know or value one's self or one's mind:

> If distress is the affect of suffering, shame is the affect of indignity, of defeat, of transgression and of alienation. Though terror speaks to life and death and distress makes of the world a vale of tears, yet shame strikes deepest into the heart of man. While terror and distress hurt, they are wounds inflicted from outside which penetrate the smooth surface of the ego; but shame is felt as an inner torment, a sickness of the soul. It does not matter whether the humiliated one has been shamed by derisive laughter or whether he mocks himself. In either event he feels himself naked, defeated, alienated, lacking in dignity or worth. (p. 118)

Shame not only breaks the social bond, it also interferes with cognition. By definition, according to Tomkins, shame involves an expectation being violated in a way that is massively dysregulating. Eyes averted, the head goes down, and we are left alone, flooded with the sense that all eyes are and should be upon us in judgment. This extreme inhibition makes it difficult to attend to or accurately read external cues. Reconnecting with others from that position of shame can be difficult. At the extreme, I have worked with individuals who were so shame prone that, even when looking in the direction of another person's eyes, the eyes remained hooded and there was no actual eye contact, merely its appearance. Concomitant with shame is a feeling of powerlessness that is experienced as further humiliation.

So, for example, I am sitting with a writer who is unable to complete any projects but rather cycles around endlessly, telling and re-telling the stories that are compelling and propel him forward but reach no satisfactory conclusion. As he tells me a story, I wonder why the character does not demand his own ending, his own course of action. In this questioning, we see how the patient—let's call him Tom—cannot find himself sufficiently to be able to find his characters. When I say something that hits home, he shifts sideways, as though avoiding being hit by something. "No," he says, then "yes," struggling between the no and the yes of it. In these moments, his aversion of gaze alerts me to his shame. Gently, I remark to him on this recurrent "no" that so often precedes his ability to reflect on ideas that are presented. "No," he says, predictably, while also considering what I am saying. We wonder together about the no—what rises up in him when he sees something about himself that he recognizes as true but also resists knowing.

I ask Tom to consider what might be the implication that he resists recognizing. Although I can recognize the resistance and highlight it for him, only he can truly speak to its meaning. What, I ask, does this statement of mine point to in him that he cannot tolerate? What does he find inside himself that is so unacceptable that he stumbles over it? Is this the stumbling that happens with his characters, too? If so, can we find a way to look at this pattern together, talk about it, and try to make sense of it? In spite of his shame, Tom is curious. As our work has progressed and our relationship evolved, he is better able to tolerate moments of shame, in part because his persistence has paid off for him in terms of greater insight.

In this small anecdote, I hope that you can see the unconscious at play, and that you can also see the analyst and the patient struggling to recognize and work with whatever bits of data become apparent, even fleetingly. There are many ways of pointing to a predicament and showing what cannot consciously be shown, whether because we *do not know it consciously* or because we are too ashamed to reveal it. And yet, it is precisely those things we stumble over—that seemingly cannot be known—that analyst and patient come together to discover. Although the analyst may recognize the stumbling, she may not know precisely what lies beyond the gap or, even if she does, the shame may have to be relieved to some extent before the material can usefully be uncovered. How we might detoxify such a moment sufficiently to be able to work together with the material rather than merely retraumatizing the patient can be a difficult technical dilemma.

In focusing on insight, Lacan shifts away from what has become a traditional view in which the purpose of therapy is "healing" or "cure." He locates the clinical conversation in *the discourse*, in this way inviting a shift in focus away from our preconceived ideas about cure and towards the events as they take place within the room. Note the similarity here to Bion's (1967b) admonition to eschew memory or desire; to avoid imposing our ideas on the situation rather than experiencing it anew. As Parsons (1986) notes, it is easy to become attached to our ideas in ways that impede our ability to encounter the present moment. Similar to theories of art that tell us that it is precisely our ability to break through our habituation and come upon something familiar anew that affords the aesthetic moment, it is important for the clinician to be able to try to meet each clinical moment with a fresh eye and ear, so that we might mine it most fully. Each moment is a new opportunity if we can be open to whatever it might offer that we had not known before, and perhaps had not yet been in a position to know. This type of openness is enhanced if we can recognize that *we* are never quite the same. Familiar moments of impasse do not necessarily mean that we are merely circling around with no progress. A more helpful metaphor, perhaps, is the spiral, in which, although we may traverse the same territory, *we* are never in exactly the same place and might find our way a bit differently based on this new perspective

If we accept the importance of eschewing memory and desire, then our role in the consulting room shifts from expert to fellow traveler. This framework implies that Freudian psychoanalysis, as practiced, may have gone off course because of a press for "cleverness" that invites us to "know the answers" and to solve problems rather than to be interested in them. In contrast to that type of practice, I would contend that the ability to be interested in our problems is at the heart of psychoanalysis and psychoanalytic psychotherapy, where there is a focus on unconscious logic rather than on conscious reason. Much like Bion, who viewed "knowledge" as a potential impediment to learning, Lacan affirmed his own faith in the process rather than in the accumulation of knowledge. For Lacan (1977a), this position was not merely a technical stance but rather an ethical one. In locating the ethics of psychoanalysis in the unconscious, Lacan points to what Bion (1977) refers to as the "truth instinct," something in us that is not content with our own dissimulation and drives towards resolution. From this perspective, the goal of psychoanalysis is inseparable from the desire of the person being analyzed. The analyst's ethics, then, are grounded in her respect for the process through which the analysand might recognize and begin to come to grips with his own desire.

Lacanians talk about *what is at stake* and, increasingly, I think that what is at stake in the consulting room is my ability to be myself and to try to speak in a way that is true to my experience *as an analyst who is also a human being.* In this way, I hope to mark the critical edge between *my desire* to understand the other person and *his ability* to know more deeply, profoundly, and truly *his own desire.* I also hope to invite the patient to take himself seriously enough to speak from the deepest parts of himself. If we think of what we know about mirror neurons, we recognize that we are inevitably communicating at a subconscious level something about our own authenticity in relation to our own deepest needs and feelings. Our ability to be true to ourselves, then, may be a fundamental anchor as the other person struggles towards and against this goal. With individuals who are locked within a prison of shame, virtually unable to encounter another, finding a meeting point can be extremely difficult.

We can consider, for example, the case of a young woman who enters the consulting room and seems to be leaving before she has arrived. She is certain she will not find with me what she is looking for. In some ways, that is the point: she believes that what she wants is literally unfindable. It has already been lost. Her presentation leaves us both casting backward towards a moment in time before all was lost. From that position, there is no place to meet in the here and now and seemingly no reason to do so. Once again, I have the not unfamiliar experience of being in the presence of someone whose eyes, in the rare moments when they meet my own, speak of utter dejection: all is lost. When all has already been lost, what is possible? This question sits in me as a point of impossibility, much as she seems to experience it. We sit together between the "all is lost" and the rush to somehow move beyond the present moment into an impossible future. My job then, I think, is to try to bring us both into a present moment where we might talk together about something that matters to the patient.

It is hard to talk to someone who is certain that all is lost, who feels so raw that almost everything feels bad, and for whom even the good moments are terrible because they cannot last. In the countertransference, I bristle against the impossible demand being made of me. I want to tell my patient what she needs to do in order to survive in a world in which there is too little and yet there might be something of value. If I can restrain this impetus sufficiently, I can then be more empathic with this person for whom the too little becomes a rubbing of salt in a wound that is too fresh and too raw to be tolerable. From that place of greater empathy, I can also be aware of how difficult it must be for my patient to tolerate sitting with her doctor, with whom she is terribly aware of the disjunction between what she had hoped to achieve in her life and where she currently finds herself. As a therapist, I try to "even the playing field" in every way I can, which comes in part from my compassion but also from a wish to not be the person my patient feels demeaned in relation to. My difficulty accepting the ways in which I am inevitably a complicit bystander denies part of the patient's dilemma and thus makes it off limits for our conversations. Owning my recognition that I do, indeed, take a part in her shame helps to bring me more present with her in the room.

One of the difficulties when dealing with malignant shame is that the aversion of gaze makes it difficult for the person to encounter something different. Even when the person dares look, she may only be able to see what she expects to see rather than encountering something different. For example, I think of one woman with a severe obsessive-compulsive disorder for whom shame kept her looking backwards for the disaster she was certain her distress must have caused. Eve told me that she avoided looking in the mirror because she was so ugly she could not tolerate seeing her own image. Eve's mother had treated her with disgust and contempt, with the result that Eve was left quite certain that she deserved such treatment. She had tried plastic surgery but still found herself hideous. I did not find her hideous, a presumption that, over time, created a disjunction between Eve's own ideas about her appearance and her growing recognition that I had a different perception. This disjunction enabled her to begin to look into the mirror beyond her initial expectation and to explore other possible ways of seeing herself. Beginning to look at herself in the mirror through new eyes helped Eve to recognize that it had been the eyes of the mother that had looked at her with such contempt that her face had become distorted and disfigured in her own eyes.

Winnicott (1971) notes that the baby looks into the mother's face and what she sees is herself. We could only conjecture what type of hatefulness Eve had encountered in the mother's gaze based on the residual self-hatred, self-contempt, and shame that had been left. The clinician often first encounters the mother's hateful gaze on the face of the patient. The expression of contempt that arises can be the first clue to the quality of those early interactions (Charles, 2004b, Chapter 3). My recognition of how profoundly Eve had internalized the mother's contempt as her own helped Eve to recognize the mother's ongoing presence in relation to herself. This perspective afforded her sufficient distance from the affect to be able to imagine the possibility of having a different relationship to herself. In addition, learning something about how self-perception develops in relation to the mother's gaze helped to provide a context in which she could understand her shame as marking meanings within the mother/daughter relationship rather than as a sign of her inherent unworthiness.

For Eve, having been unloved had become stigmata that made her feel so unlovable that she had not been able to develop healthy relationships. Instead, she had continually found herself being used by individuals who pretended to be friends. Her certainty that this pattern must be her fault increased her shame and made it even more difficult for her to make appropriate demands in relationships. Her mounting frustration and anger were also a source of shame, so much so that she could not even know that she was angry. Rather, her anger manifested in the obsessive conviction that she had killed someone without realizing it. This fear made it increasingly impossible for her to drive from one destination to another without having to go back over her trail to find the disaster she was certain she had wreaked. Once again, it was only in the context of being able to retell Eve's life story in a way in which it *made sense* to be angry that she was able to even consider the idea that she *might be* angry. Until that time, the idea that she might be angry merely felt like one more accusation of unworthiness.

Using these anecdotes as examples, we can see how shame, because it averts gaze, makes it difficult for us to look at precisely what we need to be able to face in order to move beyond the point where we are stuck. When we consider Mary, who will be described in Chapter 7, we will see an example of someone for whom encountering another person's gaze was so terrifying that she literally blinded herself as she moved towards making eye contact, her eyes hooding and slipping to the side. This aversion of gaze was also true figuratively, as she could not make sense of simple words that were too affectively loaded to be able to link them together.

So, then, as we think about the relationship of shame to the possibility of insight, we can see them in an inverse relationship. Affective intensity interferes with cognition. Intense shame can make it virtually impossible to look at whatever we most need to be able to see. It is important for the clinician to be able to recognize this dilemma and to be able to think of ways to attenuate the shame. At times, this can be done by normalizing the experience that marks the individual as worthy of contempt in her own eyes *if* we can develop our relationship sufficiently that she is willing or able to even let us in on this terrible secret. At other times, it is in the retelling of the story from another perspective that the shame is reduced and the broken interpersonal bond is repaired. Technical considerations that might help to facilitate the telling of a story that could not be told will be taken up in the following chapters.

Chapter Five

Development, Negation, and the Desire to Turn a Blind Eye

Part I

In this chapter, we will briefly consider development from the perspectives of Bion, Lacan, and Winnicott as a way of thinking about our position as therapist in relation to the patient's goals and tasks in therapy and in life. Because Bion (1977) posits the fundamental developmental challenge in terms of interest versus avoidance, he locates the Oedipal dilemma, not in terms of a sexual triangle, but rather in the more global desire to turn a blind 74 eye to whatever feels shameful. Notably, shame is not only a response to encountering a taboo but is also elicited by failures to achieve developmental milestones. Thinking, then, about Lacan's ideas regarding the Subject caught by the desire of the Other, we can see how the blind eye can be invoked by a challenge we either cannot meet or, alternatively, cannot meet without betraying ourselves (or someone else) in the process. If we take seriously Lacan's ideas about how individuals become entangled in other's desires, then we know that we, too, can easily find ourselves in the position of the well-intentioned other who invites obedience and self-betrayal. This awareness invites us to remember to step back from our own desires or ideas 75 about *how things should be* in order to listen more carefully to what we are being told. This is also the stance taken by Winnicott (1971) in *Playing and Reality*, where he positions the task of the therapist in line with the good enough parent, who tracks the course of the child as a developing subject and steps in when needed to relieve distress or offer bits of information *without* positioning herself as the expert. Winnicott offers a plea to the therapist to leave room for the patient's creative development by refraining from showing off what she knows. Reminding ourselves that our job is first to listen to the other person's dilemma as he experiences it can help us from being so reactive that we can't even agree on what it is we might be trying to do together. If I can remember that I am hired first to listen and try to appreciate the person's dilemma as she experiences it, I can more easily recognize my own acting out when it occurs.

Bion posits the fundamental developmental challenge in terms of our interest in learning versus the desire to *turn a blind eye*. Perhaps most problematic is our desire to turn a blind eye to that internal voice of conscience that he refers to as the *truth instinct*. It is easy for the clinician who feels like she is on the hot seat to forget what she knows about countertransference or to have in mind that she is likely *not* the most anxious person in the room. Under stress, we can lose touch with our internal truths and forget our responsibilities to the patient. It is relatively easy—particularly in early stages when I am trying to prove myself or in times of high distress when I am trying to keep the boat from rocking—for me to feel pulled into the role of "expert" or "supportive" or "helpful" therapist, and thus to lose my therapist mind. I might, for example, find myself relieving my own anxiety by "playing therapist" as best I can, and thus offering the patient something that he may not need in order to relieve my own distress. In such moments, it can be easy to focus on tension relief and to confuse the relief of my own anxiety with good practice. I have learned to recognize the internal signals that help to cue me when such an enactment is in place. Being able to recognize those signals helps me to pull back a bit from my own momentum so that I can be more reflective and consider what I might say to the patient about whatever we are caught in.

For example, I am sitting with a patient who is telling me, once again, about the extent of her distress and how unhelpful she finds me. Internally, I am reactive to these charges and want to repair myself in her (and my own) eyes. Over time, however, I have learned to restrain these impulses and to accept what she is saying as her dilemma. I am, indeed, not able to take away her pain. What I am able to offer her, in contrast, is some appreciation of how difficult it is to live with intense pain that goes on and on and seems as though it will have no end. Part of what I can offer is a willingness to be in the pain with her as she flails and rails against the destiny that brings her to this place. Inevitably, I must also come to grips with her resistance to this demand, and my own resistance to being experienced as the person who fails and persecutes her through my acceptance of the inevitability of the pain.

Patients come to us, in part, hoping for some "cure" or transformative event that might save them from the painful task of working at the problems that plague them. It is easy, as a therapist, to be caught up in this fantasy and to fail to see the inevitable ambivalence behind this wish. Needing us means recognizing their own limits, given that they have been unable to effect this change on their own. To fail to respect the ambivalence, resentment, and envy that can ensue when finding oneself in such a position of need leaves the therapist out of empathic attunement with the part of the patient whose narcissism is wounded by the need to seek assistance.

There is a stumbling that occurs when we reach a developmental challenge that requires us to move beyond the previous organization we had achieved. Those who work with children are familiar with the dysregulation that occurs at precisely the point when a new developmental demand is being made that taxes the child's resources and requires the development of new skills and adaptations. Bion (1977) highlights the crossroads we reach between the curiosity and interest that might lead us to negotiate the challenge, versus the part of us that might *turn a blind eye* and avoid that challenge. Good enough parenting enables the child to learn, not only to tolerate dysregulation, but also to be rewarded for this tolerance through his eventual mastery of the challenge.

For those for whom this type of challenge has meant failure and humiliation, however, hitting a difficulty feels like encountering impossibility. The desire to turn a blind eye may be seen to mark an internal choice point that we can hit without even noticing that we have made a choice. Being able to notice the blind eye in our patients can be an important marker for the therapist, who may be presented with *eyes wide shut* in a way that can obscure the dilemma. There is a particular feel to this *eyes wide shut* that I urge you to reflect on and keep in mind so that you can perhaps use this rubric as an indicator in your work. I have experienced this dilemma, in particular, with patients such as Christine, whom I will describe more fully in Chapter 8. Such individuals can be so traumatized that they are largely lost in the moment of the trauma, unable to do much more than look backward at what has been lost as though they might, somehow, live through the past moment differently. This recursive circling back through a trauma that has already occurred can be one sign of a disrupted mourning process.

Trauma not only impedes mourning, it also complicates the achievement of developmental milestones, leading to different types of resolutions. Lacan distinguishes between three different types of denial or, in Freud's terms, *negation*. Looking at the same developmental challenge described by Winnicott in terms of object usage, Lacan imposes a different language that is in some ways difficult to penetrate but can be quite useful clinically. Consistent with Bion's focus on curiosity versus avoidance, from Lacan's perspective the primary developmental achievement is to be able to tolerate Limit and Lack. From this perspective, we recognize that we are inevitably only one desiring subject in relation to other subjects, and that our desire is always conditioned by the rules and structures that govern the social surround. No one gets it all. Being limited then, demands that we recognize our own desires sufficiently to be able to prioritize them and work towards whatever satisfaction we might be able to achieve.

For Lacan, our *ideas* about these social rules fall within the realm of the Imaginary, whereas the constraints we experience as we are conditioned by the social structure fall within the realm of the Symbolic. Our own Imaginary—the world as it exists in our mind—is inevitably conditioned by the world as it is offered to us by our families and communities. Perception, as Grotstein (2000) notes, is inevitably *apperception*, which affects consensual as well as personal meanings. Tensions develop, however, between personal and the social meanings. These tensions increase and are more notable as we move out into the larger social surround beyond our family and begin to encounter differences between our *ideas* about ourselves and other people, other people's ideas, and *the way things are*. Optimally, psychoanalysis or psychoanalytic psychotherapy provides a space where these distinctions can become increasingly visible so that we can think about our own ideas in relation to those of others, as we stumble over the gaps.

This capacity to reflect on our own ideas is what is referred to as *reflective function*, a capacity that for Lacan depends on the ability to encounter another person's mind as other, in line with Winnicott's ideas about the transitional space. I am stressing the overlap between these theorists because there is something odd that happens in the psychoanalytic literature, as various theorists try to bring to life clinical realities that are difficult to capture in words. Although we may find a particular psychoanalytic language more or less accessible, we should be warned against believing that these languages necessarily point in different directions. To the contrary, if we can see the overlap, we are in a position to use these various lenses to help us define more clearly the area of study.

Lacan organizes his understanding of the developmental task of coming to grips with Limit in terms of the "Name of the Father" or the "No" of the Father, in this way organizing a triadic structure. Note that this triadic structure is similar to the play space of Winnicott, in which the separation between the child and the parent enables the child to find his way into the culture. In Lacan's terms, the Father becomes the third perspective that helps to bring the child out of the me-versus-you dichotomy, and into a structure where value is not merely a function of individual need or will but rather can be considered according to some greater rule or logic. Cantin (2002) calls this the *Trauma of Language*, the induction into a social order that limits our ability to satisfy our desire in the abstract, but also makes possible the satisfaction of particular desires.

Meeting this developmental challenge rests on our ability to tolerate frustration, a capacity that depends on sufficient external containment to be able to develop affective self-regulation. This containment is described by

Bion and Winnicott, respectively, in terms of, first, sufficient *reverie* or *holding* to be able to think about the other's needs and feelings without necessarily believing that one should solve or eradicate all problems. For Bion, the mother's reverie—her ability to both feel and think about the distress of the child—enables the child to feel recognized as a separate subject. The therapist provides this type of function through her willingness to appreciate the extent and particularity of the other person's problem and to believe that somehow *he* can meet whatever challenges living has posed. The second major challenge for the therapist is highlighted by Winnicott (1971) in his description of *the use of the object*: the mother's capacity to be used and discarded by her child and to survive. For Winnicott, our ability to maintain our position in relation to another person so that we can be reliably located—*without necessarily needing him to agree*—enables him to go off and gather his own data and return. Being able to confront and explore differences between people without feeling as though difference must be dire or lethal is in many ways a precondition for real learning to occur.

Let's pause to give ourselves an example here, looking at the separation anxiety that develops in relation to the greater independence of the child who is just beginning to crawl. If we watch a young child who is just developing the physical capacity to leave his mother, we see how he is most free to move away when he can check back and find the mother engaged in watching him. When he encounters her presence and her interest, he smiles and continues his exploration. If she becomes distracted, he might begin to make noise as a way of reassuring himself that he can get her attention. Failing that, he might move back towards her or signal his distress in some other way. At this point, the child is developing the resources, such as depth perception, that will enable him to be more competent at some of the functions for which he previously was dependent on his parents. He is not, however, independent enough to survive on his own and so, paradoxically, with greater *independence* comes greater awareness of his *dependence*, leading him to reassure himself that he is not alone. As his perceptual capacities develop, he is also discriminating between distance and absence, in this way learning to distinguish between manageable and unmanageable gaps.

Depth perception is a good model for the structure we are pointing to in the social world. Being able to see the gap between ourselves and others means that we need a way of organizing how we do and do not fit. Just as the laws of physics help to organize our expectations of our bodies in space, so the laws of Language help us to navigate the social surround. Underlying the laws of Language is Signification. Meaning depends on the endorsement of consensual agreements regarding the nature of reality. We will consider the use of Signifiers as markers of meaning in a later chapter.

For now, however, we will consider Lack as an important marker of meaning. Depending on our previous experience, this Lack may mark an insurmountable obstacle or merely a point of difficulty. From a Lacanian frame, this obstacle is seen as a cut, a gap, between what we might want and what we are able to have. Development rests on our ability to accept this fact. From a Bionian frame, we are back once again at the choice point between curiosity and the desire to turn a blind eye.

Lacan posits three different resolutions to this problem. The *neurotic* solution is to accommodate to the need to separate oneself from the mother by repressing some of our desires that are prohibited by the social structure. The neurotic accepts the conditional nature of satisfaction and tries to find a workable compromise between what he might want and what he might be able to achieve. We will leave the neurotic solution to the side in this particular volume.

The *psychotic* resolution, from a Lacanian frame, is a function of not having a clear path by which to move from the satisfactions of the dyad into a workable compromise. For Lacan, the psychotic has not been afforded sufficient ground on which to stand within the social surround. The failure of the paternal function to introduce a limit and help the person to accommodate to it leaves the psychotic individual in limbo. The failure to effectively come to grips with the inevitability of limit and of lack leaves satisfaction only in the realm of the Imaginary, where it might, somehow, magically be obtained. Without sufficient assistance, the hazard is that the person will turn towards a fantasy of infinite satisfaction rather than negotiating the developmental challenge of learning to attain more circumscribed satisfactions in relation to real others. In later chapters, we will consider some of the technical difficulties we encounter when working with individuals who are caught in that type of limbo.

The *perverse* solution, in contrast, is to deny the gap. Here again we have the paternal failure to mark a limit, but this failure comes on top of maternal satisfaction that the individual is reluctant to relinquish. As Winnicott (1984) notes, the most terrible thing that can happen to a baby is when the early relationship with the parent has been tantalizing. This type of tantalizing early environment leaves the individual with the fantasy of what Lacan calls *Jouissance*—the limitless pleasure that we imagine we might have. Giving up this fantasy paves the way for particular satisfactions of particular desires but at a price. That price may be too high to pay, making perversions in many ways the most difficult disorders to treat.

For example, in Chapter 5 we will encounter a young man who cannot meet particular demands of daily living. Pete's parents are unable to help him to tolerate frustration sufficiently to work through the obstacles he encounters and so, over time, he achieves a perverse solution by turning increasingly towards internal pseudo-resolutions. He denies failure by turning away from it, recreating the story of his life in ways that stress his precocious intelligence and obscure his inability to utilize his talents towards achievement of any real goals. He also denies relational needs by pretending, creating stories that are sufficiently engaging that he does not feel the gap left by his isolation from others. For Pete, this turning away from his relational needs and his needs for achievement decreases his frustration. The price, however, is paid dearly in terms of an ever-increasing failure to meet real developmental challenges. Those who have achieved pseudo-resolutions to their problems, as found in eating disorders, for example, achieve satisfaction in ways that allow them to continue their lives to some extent but impede further development in important ways. There is then a circling around the *symptom that has become the problem* in a way that obscures the underlying failure. As these failures mount, the denial and reliance on the perverse resolution can be exacerbated.

In some ways, pseudo-solutions that traverse too great a gap may be least accessible to change because of the fault that underlies them. This may be due in part to the instability engendered by unresolved trauma. When an individual is trying to go on in spite of a failure to negotiate and work through the traumatic experience, there remains a fault line that can destabilize any attempt to move forward. This particular type of fault line is endemic in current culture, where we have the idea that if we just tried harder and kept moving forward we could accomplish anything, without having to really recognize the price or limits of this "moving forward." Those of us who work with individuals with complex problems that are not easily solved by medication or short-term therapy can note how that type of mentality becomes a further burden to those who feel indicted by their failure to achieve relief. As therapists, then, it is important to be able to feel our own internal push towards solution as a countertransference reaction to the patient's feelings of failure. From that perspective, we are in a better position to help those individuals who tend to be marginalized to be more respectful of their needs, including the need to face the very hard work that might ultimately help them to have greater choice and a better quality of life.

It is important to be able to recognize that part of our desire to "help" people is also a desire to not have to face some of the tragedy that is part of living. We have theories that help us to recognize countertransference as a potentially useful tool. How to effectively manage the feelings that arise in us when we are sitting with someone who is so dysregulated that they are having trouble knowing or using their mind, however, can be a pragmatic difficulty that those theories do not easily address. This difficulty is part of what invites us to use diagnoses as a way of distancing ourselves from those whose development has been severely disrupted. The very tools that can help us to notice constellations of problems in ways that might constructively guide our interventions can be hazardous if these diagnostic categories become too reified in our minds.

The reification of diagnoses can result in people being seen as problems to be solved rather than as individuals who are facing difficult challenges. Being seen as a problem to be solved further complicates the individual's attempt towards recovery, particularly when the traumatic story being told through the symptom is occluded by the very diagnosis that attempts to describe where the trouble lies (Andreason, 2007; Morgan & Fisher, 2007). Humanistic values may be particularly important in our work with individuals who have become increasingly dysregulated and disorganized by the interpretations and demands of those who would ostensibly provide "care." It is very difficult to work with such an individual without becoming increasingly dysregulated one's self; thus one can well understand the impetus of caregivers to medicate symptoms or manage behaviors so as to de-escalate the level of distress. It is important, then, to be able to consider to what extent we are trying to relieve the other person's distress or our own so that we can have an honest conversation, rather than stepping to the side and using diagnosis as a way to avoid looking at the various options that might be available and discussing them respectfully with the patient. It is also important, when working under the strain of ongoing dysregulation, to have in mind Winnicott's (1971) injunction to refrain from stealing the patient's discovery by interpreting prematurely. This injunction reminds us to hold steady, to pay attention to our own position in relation to the patient, and to be respectful of the other person's capacity to learn.

As we consider these difficulties, it is important to be able to be curious about where the person is actually stuck and what they are struggling with, in their own terms. This recognition helps us to recognize our countertransference in terms of signals that might help us to address those difficulties more competently, rather than finding ourselves silenced by the limit the other person has come to. Being silenced by the limit can be particularly problematic when working with an individual who turns her own blind eye to the very problems requiring assistance, as we will consider in the next chapter.

Chapter Six

Development, Negation, and the Desire to Turn a Blind Eye

Part II: Perversion

In this chapter, we will take the concepts introduced in the last chapter and consider how they may play out clinically in our work with individuals who have achieved perverse resolutions to their problems. The perverse resolution poses particular dilemmas for the clinician. Often, these individuals do not *91* even seek psychotherapy because their solutions are working well enough. When the defenses fail, however, the clinician may be faced with an individual who is striving, not to work through the problem, but to return to the previous state of equilibrium afforded by the perverse solution. We can see this type of dilemma in addictions of all sorts. Whether the addiction is to food, alcohol, drugs, or the high that comes from self-harm, not-eating, or getting away with risky behavior, the individual often seeks to resolve the distress without giving up the habit. In the following chapter, we will consider a further iteration of negation as we turn to psychosis and discuss various clinical dilemmas we encounter when working with individuals for whom symbols have lost their signifying power and are lived rather than interpreted.

Perversion may be seen as a pseudo-resolution to an impossible problem. *92* Unlike the psychotic resolution, in which the search for meaning continues, the difficulty with perversion is that it works all too well. Efforts, then, tend ✗ to be towards maintaining the perverse resolution or restoring it when it fails. There seems to be a biochemical element to perversion. If we look at eating disorders, for example, we can think of the "high" that anorexics achieve by not eating and that bulimics achieve through the cycle of binge eating and vomiting. If we think in terms of affect regulation in relation to the deficits in what Winnicott (1971) calls the early facilitating environment, we can see the eating disorder as a perverse resolution to an impossible problem: how one might achieve affective self-regulation in the absence of sufficient maternal containment. It should be noted that the perverse resolution can be a defense against the type of psychotic process that can also be put into play by traumatic and deficient early environments (Read, van Os, Morrison, & Ross, 2005).

As an example, we can take the dilemma of the young woman who is angry that she is being asked to give up her most trusted defenses of cutting and not eating without being offered anything in their place that might relieve her terrible distress. This young woman's development was impeded by a mother whose own needs made her unreliably available and by a father who was alternatively warm and doting or hostile, aggressive, and actively abusive. This young woman tried to find her way in life by using her intelligence and creative capacities but her perverse reliance on not-needing anything or anyone and using starvation and cutting as ways to relieve her distress eventually brought her life to a standstill. The rage at encountering one's need when objects have been tantalizing and unreliable can prove lethal.

Thinking in terms of Lacan's (1978a) ideas regarding perversion helps us to recognize what may otherwise appear to be a perplexing and unrelenting impasse as, rather, a perverse resolution that has severely impeded development. Lacan describes perversion in terms of a pseudo-relationship with a fantasied other. Because there is no actual other who might insert his own needs or desires and thus make a demand, the individual is free to continue to satisfy his desire without disruption. The perverse resolution thus is self-sustaining and is further fueled by the failure to attain developmental milestones that are increasingly out of reach as the perversion becomes further entrenched. This is the addictive cycle by which the *failure* to achieve satisfaction fuels the drive rather than attenuating it because of the relief that is obtained at the level of the symptom. This type of cycle creates an alliance with the perverse object—whether that be a drug, food, cutting, or even a person—that takes the place of and precludes any real relationship between two separate and interacting beings. Many of our patients can be seen to have perverse relationships with their own pain. If we fail to appreciate the gratification associated with the pain, we are invited further into participation in the perversion rather than being in a position to recognize it and attempt to address the underlying difficulties.

Perhaps more significant than the gratification afforded by keeping a perversion entrenched can be the narcissistic injury entailed in acknowledging the need for assistance. Failing to recognize how precariously the individual's self-esteem may be positioned can lead to impasse or even a negative therapeutic reaction. This is one of those occasions when our desire to be helpful can be deadly to the treatment, particularly if we fail to recognize the more hostile and aggressive aspects of the patient that may be invited to thwart our good intentions. Dying, for such individuals, can represent a longed-for release from pain and the fulfillment of a fantasy of infinite peace or retaliation.

With patients who circle around death and dying with such recursive love and longing, I often have the sense of a religious ritual or liturgy, a communion of sorts. In these moments, it feels as though the individual is rocking in silent prayer, going through repetitive internal movements and unable to let go. I have come to think of these moments in terms of rosary beads, fingered repetitively in silent prayer. These rituals can be completely absorbing, effectively shutting out the external world.

I will offer two cases in which the repetitive internal rituals seemed to provide relief in a way that was almost addictive. The soothing, paradoxically, came through repetitive engagement with the pain. Both young women had struggled with anorexia, which produces a certain "high" that can become addictive. In some ways, their repeated cycling through the despair seemed to afford them a similar type of "high." This type of behavior can often be found in individuals who have experienced insufficient parental attunement and for whom self-regulation of emotions is an ongoing dilemma. Alice had learned to inure herself from any sense of need and to channel all of her efforts into academic and work success. Kim, in contrast, had received some maternal sustenance but the mother's love had been tainted by—and lost to—her despair. This deficit left Kim looking for a transformative effect, through art and intellectualization, that would move her beyond the need for real relationships that inevitably proved both loving and disappointing.

With Alice, for example, the rosary beads so lovingly fingered seem to mark an abstention from living *because* the pain might be too much to bear (see Charles, 2006a for a fuller explication of this case). Alice's averted gaze and relentless falling towards death mark the impossibility of imagining an other who might recognize her without catastrophe. With no one to recognize the pain and mark the rupture, the pain becomes the *most* reliable other— clung to with most fervor, most passion. The attachment to the pain takes on a perverse dimension, so that potential engagements threaten her relationship with her pain and are shut down almost as soon as she begins to be enlivened by them.

Kim, in contrast, was abandoned in early childhood by her suicidal mother. The elusive mother, whose pain obscures all else, pulls her into the realm of the Imaginary—Winnicott's "Fantasying"—that threatens to become an end in itself through which she might lose her life. For Kim, the rosary beads make of the pain a perverse object that also seems to be a move back towards the womb, a fantasy of refuge that is inevitably and terribly empty. The memory that encapsulates the relationship with the mother is one she must have been told because it occurred before she could possibly have had such a vivid memory of the scene. The scene involves the mother handing Kim over to the grandmother, knowing that she is leaving her forever. The place of the mother is both loving and deadly, in her choice of death as the ultimate solution to pain. For Kim, too, there is a perverse relationship with the pain that has become equated with mother.

With individuals such as Alice and Kim, the impasse in which they are caught tends to be reenacted in the therapeutic relationship. The clinician all too easily finds herself in increasing opposition to the patient. When we find ourselves desperately feeling as though we are fighting for the life of someone who is heading in the opposite direction, that is a cue that can inform us that we are playing out one half of the patient's ambivalence. This type of splitting also alerts us to the extent of the trauma that can fragment meaning, particularly under conditions of stress, and disrupts development more broadly.

If we think of trauma as a rupture that fragments meaning, we see how the impasse marks the meanings that cannot be held, and therefore also marks the Law that does not hold. The instability *becomes* internal: When we are too flooded with emotion, we literally cannot take in information. For those with histories of profound dysregulation, it can be difficult to find sufficient grounding during hard times to be able to hold steady and to feel as though one can survive the moment *without* disappearing in some fashion. When the parents have been unable to help the child stay within—or even come back to—manageable limits, this failure in *external* containment makes it difficult to achieve the type of *internal* self-regulation so important to normal development. When neither parent can be relied on to mark the difficulties and try to repair them, it is hard to imagine how help might be forthcoming. At that point, there is no "third"; no assurance that meaning can be *found* and *held* between people in any way that might make life worth living.

This lack of consensual understanding can erase not only the type of boundaries that govern and make safe social relationships, but also aspects of history, as Davoine and Gaudillière (2004) have highlighted. At such times, deficits are experienced as *internal* rather than in terms of the type of *structural trauma* LaCapra (1999) describes that marks a deficit within the social fabric. The designation of "victim" adds to the personal sense of deficit and shame, making it even more difficult to come forward and take a stand (Charles, 2000). Recognizing the price of identifying oneself as a victim can be an important turning point that helps the person fight to make a different choice in moments of strain.

In therapy, then, we try to find a way to help the traumatized individual locate herself as a valued subject so that she might bring into language whatever has been dissociated and thus left to speak in another register through the symptom. We also see, however, that her agency is entangled with a hatred for being thus reduced. If we fail to take seriously this dilemma—that requiring assistance can feel shaming and thus invoke retaliatory hostility—we run the risk of trying to be actively "helpful" or "supportive" rather than providing a space in which the person can struggle with her *very real ambivalence* regarding what it might mean to turn away from death and face living.

From a Lacanian perspective, there is no way to define the Subject or to come to terms with one's own subjectivity without a confrontation with lack and with limit. For Alice and Kim, this confrontation was too profound and too early. They managed to survive through their intelligence and creative accomplishments, but over time the austerity of these resolutions wore through and life became increasingly empty and meaningless. The austerity that had helped them survive now pulled them relentlessly and virulently towards death.

Dissociating and denying bodily or relational needs seemed to offer escape from their impossible dilemmas. They each sought a state of needlessness that would offer, not only respite from pain, but also the type of transcendence that LaCapra (1999) points to in his depiction of structural trauma. The danger in this type of resolution is that, in the attempt to move beyond the pain, one may not actually come to grips with whatever has been causing it. In this way, the attempt to deal with the symptom rather than the underlying cause creates a self-defeating cycle. Further complicating this dilemma and perhaps most difficult, clinically, is the attachment to the pain.

For both Alice and Kim, maternal failures and paternal attacks left them oddly disembodied, attempting to tell a story they in some sense did not even know. When trauma has impeded self-knowledge, the symptom of dissociation can be seen as a statement regarding the dilemma of the person in relation to herself. At that point, the therapist potentially becomes the witness who can both empathically enter the experience and also remain separate, so that as Felman (1995) puts it: "the knowledge [that] *does not exist,* . . . can *happen*" (p. 53). There is always the hazard with individuals so ensconced in self-denial, however, that being afforded a witness to the pain will merely add to the gratification.

Further complicating these types of sadomasochistic enactments is the tendency in North American culture to devalue the feminine and to subordinate emotions and the body in ways that pathologize distress and increase *dis*order (Charles, in press). In line with Bion's (1987) idea of "Emotional Turbulence," we see Alice and Kim poised at the brink of an autonomous development they have not quite been able to manage. Each is willing to forsake her body, and even her life, but not her creative potential. Each has reached a point of impasse where what previously helped keep her alive—her ability to write—became an unsatisfactory substitute for living. What had previously "fed" them had become empty and meaningless. How then, can they move beyond the impasse? How do they tolerate dependence enough to rely on someone else while building their own resources, which would mean struggling with the type of annihilation anxiety noted clinically by Klein (1946) and also affirmed by research data (Benveniste, Papouchis, Allen, & Hurvich, 1998). Such efforts would also require tolerating the shame and narcissistic injury they experience when they acknowledge their dependency needs.

There is often a very slim line between being able to negotiate a working therapeutic relationship with such an individual versus finding oneself embroiled in a sadomasochistic and perverse enactment. I find it at times impossible to tell which side of this line I am on in a given moment and can only hope that my efforts will be used by the patient in the service of their development rather than in the service of further fueling the perversion. In such moments, I often speak to this hope as a way of affirming to the patient both my position and their power.

As an example, let's take the case of a young woman whose extensive and severe trauma history left her with an intense need/fear dilemma in which she desperately wished to rely on others but was terrified of doing so. Her experience had left her feeling outside of the social structure and particularly suspicious about relying on anyone in authority. The developmental achievement of basic trust had never been accomplished.

Although Mara led with her sincere desire to make full use of her treatment, these efforts would be waylaid by competing demands that often came in the form of somatic complaints or loyalty binds with peers. It was difficult to speak with her about my sense that she was leading with her good intentions and then allowing her ambivalence to play out indirectly rather than bringing it more explicitly into the consulting room. I knew from her history that she was a very good liar, which left me further adrift from her as I found myself unable to separate honesty from earnest attempts to be believed.

An opportunity to open up this conversation came in the form of a lie that was incontrovertible. Mara was talking about issues of truth and lies that were coming up in her social world and, once again, affirmed her truthfulness. I said that I thought it might be a bit more complicated than that, and gave as an example the incident that had occurred and referred to her lie as an "embellishment." She lit up, delighted at hearing recognition, without attack, of a part of herself with which she was all too familiar. "Embellishment," she replied, "I like that word." By offering her my recognition, without judgment or attack, of something that is complicated about her and interferes with her relationships, I was able to invite Mara to work with me at trying to better understand this part of herself.

Mara's relief at being recognized without being judged helped her to become more forthright and direct with me. She began to trust that I might be someone who could be relied upon. This reliance, built on our developing recognition that my role was *not* to take care of or manage her but rather to bring issues to her attention, helped her to bring problems into our work that she knew I would be concerned about. Our work together enabled Mara to build sufficient trust that, over time, she was able to use me more directly as a resource through which to better understand herself and to work towards her goals.

With Pete, in contrast, this was not possible. Pete's ambivalence expressed itself through the various lies he would tell and the tests he would devise to ascertain to what extent I was worth trusting. There were times when I would only become aware of such a test when he would report that I had passed or failed. At other times, I would recognize that a test was being created and refuse to participate. I told him that I was not interested in playing games or proving that I was clever. To the contrary, I told him, it was not cleverness that I valued but rather honesty. I took a strong stand advocating for integrity as the lynch pin of the treatment. If he really wanted this treatment to be different from those he had managed to sabotage in the past, he would need to be honest.

To his credit, Pete did try to be honest, bringing in some of his more difficult truths, including sharing secrets from some of his old journals. Doing so, however, was so disorganizing that his reactions were at times quite violent, such that subsequent sessions could be spent quite masterfully trying to erase or obscure the painful truth that had been revealed. It was so difficult for him to tolerate being known that he would often obscure truth almost as soon as it was revealed, hiding any painful admission behind a later retraction and even displaying different persona as he dodged and hid from view.

Eventually, we came to what Pete described as a turning point. He reported that he felt like running away from the truths that we had opened up. He said that he knew that if he ran away now there was likely no turning back. He saw this moment as a choice point between the arduous work that would be entailed in trying to face himself honestly without the lies and deceptions he had relied on so heavily, versus continuing to build the false persona he has chosen to hide behind. We were both sad when he chose to leave. I was also angry. In that anger, I could recognize Pete's parting shot of hostility, through which I could recognize that his engagement in the work had always been a pseudo-engagement. "Doing a good job at it" was an important pretense to achieve for many pragmatic reasons, in part to enhance his self-esteem and in part to keep his parents on the hook paying for his treatment and his keep. However, as he could acknowledge quite directly, actually working hard was something he had never been good at and did not want to tackle now. In that determination, we could see how his narcissistic investment in appearance over substance left him further and further away from achieving any goals he could actually be proud of, aside from the gratification he experienced from managing to fool and use people in the service of achieving his current aims.

When perversion is entrenched, our best therapeutic efforts can be commandeered into a perverse engagement. Even when substantial gains are made, as was the case with Alice, the perverse element can be virulent and relentless. Alice, for example, was able to achieve a great deal through our work together that helped her move forward in her professional development and build healthier relationships. As time went by, however, her dependency on me did not relieve. It seemed to me that we were caught in a perverse engagement in which she needed to be ill enough that she did not have to relinquish her dependence. I talked with her about my sense that she needed to move on, and wondered aloud about her fears of gaining greater autonomy. We explored her inhibitions. Eventually, however, this self-destructive dependency continued and I initiated a termination of our work together. I had encouraged Alice to find another therapist with whom to discuss this perverse and dangerous dependency that seemed to sustain her self-destructive behaviors. I found out later, when she contacted me to report how well she was doing and to thank me for my efforts on her behalf, that she had not found a new therapist but rather had used the support network she had been building at work to sustain her in more adaptive ways. Although I was concerned about how her self-destructiveness might fester without direct attention, I hoped that our work together had been sufficient that she would be able to ask for help if she needed it.

This type of impasse is very difficult to work with. We can't necessarily control how another person uses us and, from my perspective the clinician's job is not to manage behavior but rather to pay sufficient attention to be able to offer our observations in ways that might be useful. When working with individuals suffering from chronic or early trauma, experiences that have been lodged in the body are often spoken directly through action or symptom rather than language (Charles, 2002b). It is challenging to hold open a space in which the person might find a way to claim a life, without making a *demand* that leaves no room for them to find their own desire. So then, how do we work with such people? How do we offer an opportunity they might actually be able to make use of? Such work, I believe, requires having some idea of what we are up against. We will take up these issues again in later chapters as we consider the *passage into action*, *empty speech*, and *attacks on linking*.

Chapter Seven

Working with Trauma

Attacks on Linking and Empty Speech

In this chapter, we use Bion's (1967c) ideas about *attacks on linking* and Lacan's (1977a) ideas about *empty speech* as lenses to help us grapple with differences encountered in work with individuals who have suffered from intrusion versus neglect. Although intrusive acts are more clearly recognizable as problems, we can see from the attachment literature the devastating effects of neglect. The depressed or unavailable parent fails to recognize the child as a subject in her own right, with needs, feelings, and desires worth attending to. In the histories of individuals who suffer from more severe disorders, we find references to feeling as though one's own needs were either invisible or more actively overridden by the needs of the parents (Charles, Clemence, Newman, & O'Loughlin, January, 2010). We have already encountered Bion's ideas about the developmental importance of being able to link ideas with one another, and have seen how trauma can interfere with this process. We have also encountered Lacan's ideas regarding the importance of recognizing the Subject's dilemma in relation to herself, and of taking seriously her need to confront, come to grips with, and learn to live with her life as it has been. There is always a story being told and untold. It becomes important to be able to listen deeply so that we can perhaps hear beyond the surface appearance to whatever meanings are being expressed less explicitly. For Lacan, one way of thinking about this paradox is to notice the type of empty speech that seems to have meaning but covers over something else. Being able to take seriously our own reaction to speech that from one perspective *sounds fine*, but from another *feels empty*, can be an important clinical clue. In the next chapter, we will consider ways in which these dilemmas, unresolved, leave the individual caught in time, having survived something she does not know how to survive.

We will continue our discussion of Alice and Kim as we consider how Bion's (1967c) ideas about *attacks on linking* and Lacan's (1977a) ideas about *empty speech* might help us work with individuals who have suffered from intrusion versus neglect. In looking at these cases through the lens of Lacan's ideas about Lack, Limit, and the importance of the Third, we can consider these women's dilemmas in the context of their developmental struggles. Growing up in households in which parental deprivation and attacks left the children open to boundary violations that took whatever love and care they felt for one another made those bonds inaccessible as sources of real comfort. When the parents fail to hold essential boundaries between right and wrong, and between self and other, it becomes very difficult for the child to recognize real limits and thus to be able to attend adaptively to real needs for safety and sustenance. In such circumstances, as we will see in the cases of Alice and Kim, the individual can become fragmented and unable to *know*, to perceive information that would be vital in making sense of dangers, real and imagined. In our work together, each repeatedly came up against the limits of what she could *usefully* know. Part of the work then, involves the clinician's ability to perceive what the patient cannot know but needs to know, to be able to hold this information, and then to help her to discover a way to encounter it herself without falling into bits.

In Bion's terms, this confrontation can be seen as an *attack on linking* in which meaning cannot be made from the facts as they are perceived and experienced. There is a part of us that resists knowing more than we can tolerate. Although this resistance can be adaptive in moments of acute distress, warding off painful knowledge over time can keep us locked in limbo, unable to integrate the information and move on. Because of this internal resistance to encountering traumatic memory, the therapist is in a difficult position, as the patient tells us in bits and pieces whatever it is that they are having trouble consciously recognizing. The person may be able to discuss information during one session that they then cannot even acknowledge in another. For example, with Alice, there were times when the abuse she had suffered was "off the table," so to speak, even though she had previously told me about it. For me, coming up against this type of wall was disorganizing and disorienting, as though I did not know what I thought I knew. At such a moment, being able to see this process of knowing and not knowing in action—and to recognize it as a symptom of trauma—was critical to any effort to find a way to work with the patient rather than opposing her limits in that moment. When encountering such intense

ambivalence, it is easy to find myself taking one side of the ambivalence as
the patient takes the other, rather than acknowledging the ambivalence in a
way that helps the person recognize it as her own.

Recognizing such a process at play requires our ability to step back a bit
and observe ourselves in action. Bion (1977) noticed that a focus on content
can obstruct our ability to track the underlying processes at work. He devised
his grid as a way of pointing to the process itself, noting that careful attention
to the sequence of events in relation to one another offers essential clues
regarding ways in which meanings are construed, constructed, and responded
to by the individual. The same words can serve very different functions,
depending on the context. This insight can be very helpful as we try to
understand a particular clinical dilemma. For example, the statement "I don't
see" can be used as a denial of meaning or as a request for information. "I
can't do it" can be a statement about one's capacities, a request for
assistance, or a refusal to budge. Being willing to inquire into the meaning of
a given statement helps keep open the possibilities in a way that can be very
helpful when we are feeling overwhelmed by what seems to be a refusal to
think but may be a statement of fact that still has some play in it. Our ability
to be interested in what the person means at that moment helps keep us
feeling alive in times of confusion or despair.

Ambivalence can be a positive prognostic sign of struggle within the
individual. At times, we are struck by the discrepancy between the story
being told and the feelings we experience when sitting with that person. This
type of discrepancy can be an important clue guiding us to investigate
further. Our willingness to investigate, to try to see what works well and also
what does not work well for a given individual, conveys an important
statement about hope and possibility. This willingness to move forward even
in the face of uncertainty can help the person to recognize and utilize his
strengths in the service of coming to grips with and learning to more
effectively work with his vulnerabilities. This stance also affirms the
therapist's belief that the answers lie in the patient.

Our patients come to us because they find themselves unable to use their
resources sufficiently to be able to move forward in their lives in some
fundamental way. For those whose histories have been marked by severe
trauma, there is a gap between the person's capacities and the ability to use
those capacities adaptively. Although the person complains of that gap, and
fights to override it, it is often that very gap that marks the problem and
invites us to look further. The gap insists that something happened that is too
important to be glossed over. From the perspective of a psychoanalytic
therapist, impasses can only be understood in relation to the individual's life
story. Trauma can be experienced in the form of an attack or as a profound
absence of containment and soothing. For many individuals who come to
such an impasse, there have been both.

Increasingly, the literature points to the fundamental importance of attachment relationships in early development. Gene by environment interaction studies show that vulnerable children can have a very good prognosis with good early care, and that early deficiencies can be moderated by later care (Schwandt et al., 2010). Taking seriously the importance of social inclusion can help the clinician to recognize and attend to the multiple layers of vulnerability for those whose early life did not afford the type of empathic attention and "marked mirroring" (Mayes, Fonagy, & Target, 2007) that has been found to be so crucial to the development of healthy self-regard. At the extreme, we can see how social exclusion has been linked to the development of psychotic spectrum disorders (Schreier et al., 2009). In our own study listening to the narrative of individuals who have been designated "psychotic," we find descriptions of *attacks and intrusions* in the context of a fundamental *absence* of parental containment (Charles, Clemence, Newman, & O'Loughlin, January, 2010).

These early interactions also impact our ability to regulate our own affect. Too much chaos in early childhood interferes with the development of the capacity for self-regulation that seems to be our fundamental self-righting mechanism in times of stress. I have found, in working with individuals who have become severely waylaid in their lives, that attending to equilibrium and disequilibrium can help the individual to develop a greater capacity for attending effectively to internal and external cues as a way of more competently managing their own affect. Being able to mark a moment of "too much" is an important first step towards recognizing that type of moment as a prompt for greater self care as a way of coming back into equilibrium, rather than continuing with whatever sequence had been put into place in the absence of that capacity. Building this capacity for affective self-regulation seems to be at the heart of therapies such as dialectical behavior therapy (DBT), where the focus is explicitly on building the person's capacity to recognize and competently manage internal cues as a way of relieving distress.

When working with people who are in extreme distress, it is easy to want to "help" in a way that invites us to try to take over and "solve" the person's problem, to fix something. At such moments, it is easy for the therapist to lose her own place and forget that she is there to assist in a process and *not* to fix something or someone. This question of how we position ourselves is a question of value: of ethics. Lacan (1977b) talks very explicitly about the ethics of the analyst in terms of a recognition of our place in the process. In his view, we are there to provide an opportunity for the other person by observing them and saying something about what we see. It is not the interpretation that is important but rather the listening, itself, thus making the integrity of the analyst critically important, as we try to listen for what might be present beyond what we already believe we know (Lacan, 1977c). In much the same way, Bion (1967b) talks about abstaining from the memory or desire that might get in the way of the kind of moment by moment tracking that might actually help people see themselves in action a bit more clearly. Given that we are always ambivalently torn between our desire to be able to just do what we've always done versus the need to work at changing, what the psychoanalytic therapist has to offer is not some sort of assistance that solves "the problem" but rather observations that help us to focus more directly on those problems, whatever they might be. The more clearly we can see ourselves in action, the better able we might be to get some traction that helps us to grapple more effectively with the facts of our existence.

Part of what we need, as psychodynamic therapists, is to be able to hear the person's story sufficiently that we can begin to note the disjunctions, the gaps, and points of impasse. Part of the utility of projective tasks, like the TAT, is that they give us the form of the story in a way that the form itself registers—the ways in which the elements are tied together in relation to one another. Being able to recognize the form of the story helps do exactly what Bion's grid points us towards: to see the underlying dilemma rather than getting so caught up in the content. We don't always have projective tests to point the way. What we do have then, are the stories people tell us that have their own organizational flow. Being able to recognize the patterns of each individual's stories is the training we need in order to be able to help that person to see what she is telling us without quite noticing.

If we can notice the story as story, we can think about the relations between individuals and between elements. We can begin to notice what is too present and also where the gaps are. Where is the vitality? Whereas one individual may be disorganized by liveliness, another may more actively kill it off. The story is always an assertion and also a hypothesis: this is how the world works. Our patients' stories tell us what is known and also what is unknown, that alerts us to something missing that might be needed in order to build a life. Thus, in the transference, we look for the details in which life *might* be grounded.

For those whose development has been disrupted by trauma, the gaps become particularly important, as we will see when we consider Lacan's ideas about *empty speech* and Bion's ideas about *attacks on linking*. As noted in the previous chapter, trauma fragments meaning, which helps us to survive but can leave us crippled and unable to put the pieces of our lives together sufficiently to make sense of our own life stories and move on with our lives. As we approach the territory of the trauma, our increasing dysregulation can make it difficult for the experience to result in anything but further dysregulation. Finding ways to enter this traumatic arena without merely retraumatizing the patient can be a difficult task, particularly with individuals for whom engagement can be so dangerous.

Returning now to Alice and Kim, each of these women long for relationships that seem inevitably out of reach. For Alice, the possibility of engagement is barred by the *im*possibility of redemption for her own crimes (see Charles, 2006a, 2007 for a further explication of this case). Meaning breaks down and fragments in relation to crimes that can neither be affirmed nor acknowledged, much less atoned for or redeemed. Kim, in contrast, anchors meaning in the productions she can no longer create, moving relentlessly into the beautiful abstractions that became so empty that they are no longer worth living for.

Further complicating the dilemma is the tendency for both Alice and Kim to disappear as a Subject. If you recall, when the confrontation with lack and limit occurs too early, attempts at survival can be brittle and wear thin. This was the case for both Alice and Kim, whose many accomplishments became increasingly empty and meaningless as the very austerity that had helped them to survive now pulled them relentlessly towards death. The attempt to transcend the pain did not afford sufficient opportunity to confront or resolve the underlying problems. In addition, cutting and starving themselves provided physiological relief from their distress, a relief that was difficult to give up, further entrenching their difficulties.

This type of impasse is very difficult to work with. The therapist must try to hold open a space in which the person might find a way to claim a life, without making a *demand* that leaves no room for her to find her own desire. In such situations, we are easily invited into a perverse engagement in which we find ourselves on one side or the other of the patient's ambivalent desire to live and to die. Although each of these women disappears as a subject, the mode of disappearance is not the same, and so is worked with quite differently. With Alice, there is a critical absence of the mother in the moment of flooding, so that the fundamental issue is one of self-regulation. She needs to learn to tolerate those terrible moments in which all hope and meaning collapse through the embodied memory of the passage into action— the point where *she* disappeared. For Kim, this issue is more ephemeral: catching the ghost of meaning—the abstraction after the fact—what has been lost without even knowing and thus is always at risk, not of ebbing away, but of having already ebbed away. This type of confusion between past and present is what Winnicott (1963/1989) highlights in his consideration of the fear of the breakdown that has already happened, marking the posttraumatic tendency towards vigilance that can feel as though the danger is imminent when it is not.

The passage into action implies the Law not holding, and also a failure to mourn (Bentolila, 2007). One cannot mourn what cannot be acknowledged. For Alice, there was no way to hold either parent accountable. The Law is held by the lawless father in relation to a mother who cannot know the truth ("she just slept through it," she says, "nothing could wake her up"). As Alice describes it, the mother's hysterical style moves from not-knowing to feeling victimized if she is forced to know. In alignment with the mother, Alice is left needing no one to know *but also*, somehow, for the other to have in mind what she can and cannot manage, which implies a perspective outside of the relationship. In the transference, my dilemma has been how do I know *anything* without imposing this awareness on her; how do we build a structure in which meaning *might be held* without her breaking into bits. For Alice, the disintegration pulls her into alliance with the fragmented mother in relation to the father who could, literally, break her into bits. Needing nothing seems to be the one refuge in a world where connection is dangerous and reality unstable.

There had been no room for two women in Alice's home of origin, and her mother's reaction to any success on Alice's part had been either to withdraw and abandon her, or to take on the success as her own. In either case, Alice disappears as a subject. In the consulting room, we can see how self-regulation becomes a fundamental issue, in relation to the critical absence of the mother in the moment of affective flooding. Our task, then, is to try to tolerate the moments in which all hope and meaning collapse through the embodied memory of the passage into action—the point where *she* disappeared.

For Kim, in contrast, the father was missing as a containing presence. He could *register* the Law; what was right and what was wrong, but was not able to anchor these rules in the pragmatics of daily life. He accused the mother, but could not register or remediate his own failures. The trauma for Kim was her mother's terrible depression that left her not only utterly unavailable to the family, but ultimately absent altogether. In the place of the mother, for Kim, is not only her mother's terrible absence but also her sense that her father had held Kim to blame. It had seemed as though it was Kim's neediness rather than the mother's incapacities that had resulted in the mother's untimely death.

At one level, both Alice and Kim describe being lost in relation to a father who attacked her and a mother who could not save her. In Alice's case, however, saving herself had meant abandoning her siblings, thereby standing accused in her *own* eyes of being just as bad as the parents. For Kim, saving herself had meant moving off into the Imaginary realm inhabited by her loving but depressed mother who, in spite of her best intentions, was not able to fight for her *own* life sufficiently for the daughter to be able to claim *hers*. For Alice, the mother is grotesque and unreliable: crazily demanding and dependent, or utterly absent. There is not even an insufficient mother upon which to construct a real other who does not fragment and come apart. For Kim, there is the lovely *representation* of a mother, loving but elusive, so that moving towards her means moving towards death. Whereas Alice defends against the descent into psychotic disintegration, which is where she locates her mother, Kim's identification is with the mother who chooses death.

Alice describes being attacked directly by a Lawless father; Kim felt undermined by the father who, in using intellectualized defenses to manage impossible feelings, became the critical other who marked Kim's own point of impossibility. In both of these families, there was no "Third," no external point of reference by which the parents could be judged in relation to their jobs as parents. Failing this reference point, each woman was foundering, unable to create a coherent narrative in which living could be seen as worth the fight; or even envision a self worth fighting for.

Each presents with something that is known and something that is unknown, something missing that might be needed in order to build a life. For Alice, what is missing is the voice of the mother, the Law that might have registered the father's lawlessness and marked his transgressions, to catch him in the act and hold in mind the violation. It is the failure to hold in mind the *fact* of the rupture that makes of it what Lacan (1962-63) calls the "*passage into action*" that retraumatizes, rather than an *enactment* out of which meaning might be made. Bentolila (2007) notes that the passage into action differs from an enactment in that it is not reversible. Something has been done that cannot be undone. There is a rupture that cannot so easily be repaired by bringing it into words.

For Kim, the passage into action was the mother's relentless depression that, although it is "known," what is missing is the *meaning* of this event regarding the mother's affective absence during Kim's infancy and her willingness to abandon her daughter. Although she was ostensibly present in the stories passed along to her daughter, in which she is depicted as lovely and loving, what was absent—even in the stories, in which she was glorified—was her *will*; the determination to hold on to life that might have become a foundation for her daughter to build on. Thus, in the transference, with Kim, we look for the details in which life *might* be grounded. With Alice, in contrast, we look for the missing voice of the mother through which she might find or build some sustenance that does not fragment and come apart in the very act of seeking it.

For each of these young women, setting themselves free from their internalized drama would mean condemning—or failing to condemn—a part of the parent they can also find within themselves, and *also* giving up the libidinized relationship with their own pain. When working with individuals suffering from chronic or early trauma, experiences that have been lodged in the body are often spoken directly through action or symptom rather than language (Charles, 2002b). Alice, for example, often "spoke" silently, through her denial of her needs, her "silent screams" that at times wracked her face, and the ways in which she positioned herself in her relationships as the person who must give and can never take. So then, how do we work with such individuals? How do we offer an opportunity they might actually be able to make use of? Such work, I believe, requires having some idea of what we are up against. So, I offer you a few ideas that I find useful in appreciating—and thereby tolerating—some of these difficulties.

ATTACKS ON LINKING

Through his work with traumatized individuals, Bion (1967c) coined the term *attacks on linking*, noting how difficult it can be to work with someone with whom the linking of two objects or two thoughts can feel so treacherous that these links are attacked and destroyed. For me, this destructive process has made working with Alice feel like being in the movie *Groundhog Day*, where the main character lives through each day only to find himself back at the beginning once again. With Alice, my experience of Groundhog Day is of working diligently to build a relationship together, obtaining some success, and then finding that whatever gains have been made have disappeared once again the following day. In such moments, it is as though whatever has happened the previous day is erased and we must begin again. Over time, however, the knowledge that whatever is built will disappear wields its own force in the room.

Alice circles around a story that must and cannot be told, first accusing her parents for failing her but then ultimately accusing herself for not having been up to the task of saving herself. Her unworthiness to even have a life is a matter of certainty, something she comes up against most notably when anything good happens. At these times, it is as though something relentless and virulent in her takes over; anything good becomes bad, any possibility is defeated. It is after our richest and deepest engagements that Alice is most likely to return the following day utterly shut down, certain that nothing good ever could or would come from such conversations. Knowing this pattern does not make her experience of it any less dire or deadly, nor does it necessarily help the therapist to maintain her balance in such a moment when object constancy has failed and there is no way to meaningfully link ourselves with one another.

Although Alice is very bright and sees our work as an opportunity to perhaps finally work through the impasse she had come to, knowing that and doing it are two very different things. It seems to be only when she is able to defeat the treatment, whether by starving herself or otherwise jeopardizing her health or livelihood, that she is able to obtain sufficient distance to be able to think about what she had been learning and to apply it for herself. We seem to waver between her absolute reliance on me and her determination to kill herself or otherwise utterly sabotage our work together. It is precisely at those times when it seems as though she has successfully killed me off as a potential resource, but has managed not to kill herself, that we can see how fundamentally she was playing at achieving the developmental milestone that Winnicott (1971) points to in his paper on "object usage." Killing me off and seeing that I could survive and still be present for her was an important precondition for discovering how to make use of me in our sessions, rather than repeating the pattern of becoming so frightened that she would increasingly shut down the more we became engaged with one another. In our sessions, I work on helping her to tolerate her distress and to hold in mind that I am not *only* the angry, hateful, critical person she experiences me to be. We work on building an *idea* of a reflective space for her to try to hold in mind when it shuts down and nothing is left but chaos and despair.

EMPTY SPEECH

With Kim, in contrast, I encounter a slipperiness that I have come to see as a façade of engagement that masks an underlying sea of chaos and fragmentation. Lacan (1977a, 1978c, d) refers to the "empty speech" that can mark the place of something that cannot be articulated directly. Empty speech skims over the surface, leaving virtually no ripple, inviting us to fail to recognize the meaninglessness, and thus introducing a note of perversity into the dyad. Being able to notice, often in retrospect, that one has been lulled into complicit acceptance of something that has no meaning can be an important call to action. I find it difficult, however, to recover in such a moment because I believe that *I have failed to do something that I should have been doing.* Learning to recognize that feeling of failure as a signal that I should inquire into the gap is an ongoing struggle for me.

We at times encounter this type of gap or empty speech in a compulsive repetition of traumatic scenes that may be an attempt to deliver an alternate end to the story rather than enduring the distress, but can also take the form of what I call "rosary beads," the fingering of which can become an end in itself. Ritualizing the traumatic event takes it out of the realm of terrible realities *to be suffered* in that it transforms the suffering into an ecstatic state that has its own rewards. At one and the same time, we live through the event and deny it, replacing loss with a mythic absence whose reality is denied (LaCapra, 1999). In contrast, in breaking through a moment of empty speech, we create an opportunity to look deeper into whatever has eluded language, including what it means to be in relation to an other.

Kim's well put together appearance is at odds with the massive collapse that resulted in her being asked to withdraw from her professional program, in spite of her stellar academic achievement. It is as difficult to locate her as an embodied being as it is to build a story in which her collapse makes sense, and I wonder how we might make sense of the discrepancies in this picture that she both presents and covers over. As I try to resonate to Kim's meanings and learn her language, I bump up against meanings I cannot decipher, and feel as though I am failing. I then easily fall into the trap of trying to overcome the gap by assiduous attention to my work, as though if I just listened harder or had more wisdom, if only I could be Other, then everything would be all right. In counterpoint to Kim's dilemma, I find *myself* in the position of the insufficient object. Once I can locate myself there, I can wonder to what extent I am identifying *with* her, or being cast as the reciprocal in her story. We are each caught between the absence *and* abusiveness of each parent, and Kim's belief that she *should* be able to "do better" even though she cannot. At a deeper level, we can see how Kim becomes lost in the belief that she cannot afford to have needs or feelings because her feelings *did not matter* enough to her mother to have kept her mother alive. As she begins to face this lack, we can begin to see her relentless move towards emptiness as an attempt to find the mother where she never was but should have been.

Kim's relentless movement towards death is both an accusation and an attempt to point to the place of the missing mother. In her own way, Alice points to this absence as well. In this process, Alice first relies on me as the person who can envision that living might be possible, then resents my intrusion, eventually pushing me out of the way, and making room for herself. Finding the hole she falls through, and filling it with some intention that can be sustained, is an arduous and in some ways heartbreaking achievement. For Alice, life imposes itself as something she *might* choose. For Kim, that choice remains elusive, as she struggles with the psychotic disorganization that ensues as she tries to grapple with the inevitable interdependence on others that would be required if she were to imagine actually living her life. For each of these young women, finding a reliable other on whom to depend without losing touch with her own needs or feelings is an arduous process, one that requires continuing commitment and a willingness to search behind the empty speech for meanings that can be coherently linked together. We will continue our discussion of working with fragmented meanings in the next chapter.

Chapter Eight

Passage into Action and the Fear of Breakdown

In this chapter, we will consider Lacan's ideas about the *passage into action* as a way of recognizing a particular difficulty we can encounter when working with traumatized individuals. The *passage into action* is similar to an *enactment* with one fundamental difference. An enactment tells a story that cannot be told in words. Being able to tell the story changes the story. In the passage into action, in contrast, something has occurred that is not reversible. We see this, for example, in the case of suicide attempts that for some reason misfire and people find themselves accidentally alive after having taken what is really an irreversible action: choosing to die and acting on this choice. Behaving in violent ways towards oneself or others can break through an inhibition in a way that eases the path towards breaking through again. Being violated by others is also an irreversible action. We can come to terms with it, but we cannot undo it. How we deal with something impossible that *has already happened* is a very difficult clinical dilemma that Winnicott (1963/1989) discusses in his idea about the *fear of the breakdown that has already happened*. To illustrate, we will consider the case of a young woman whose experience left her unable to make sense of the events in her live or even, at times, the words of others.

I will use a case previously reported in order to consider from another perspective Winnicott's (1963/1989) ideas regarding the "fear of breakdown" that *has already happened* (Charles, 2004a, 2006b). Although the term breakdown can be used in many ways, Winnicott speaks particularly in reference to psychotic phenomena. He describes psychosis in terms of a reversal of the maturational process that occurs in an environment in which one cannot rely on others upon whom one is, indeed, dependent. In such instances, he suggests, the defenses normally in place against the breakdown of the unit self fail and ego organization is threatened. Much like Bion (1967a), Winnicott contends that we all have within us the potential for such an unthinkable state of affairs, and that our normal defenses invite us to particularize what is likely a universal capacity in order to relieve our own fears. Being able to recognize this fear—and, along with it, this commonality—makes it possible for the clinician to be more empathic to the patient's terror and to tolerate his dependence during moments of extreme dysregulation.

Winnicott (1963/1989) contends that the types of "primitive agonies" (p. 88) that are associated with psychosis are not seen clinically. What we see, rather, is only the defense organization because "the underlying agony is unthinkable. It is wrong to think of psychotic illness as a breakdown; it is a defence organization relative to a primitive agony, and it is usually successful (except when the facilitating environment has been not deficient but tantalizing, perhaps the worst thing that can happen to a human baby)" (p. 88). Note how, in this passage, we see Winnicott's fundamental agreement with Lacan regarding the difficulty of treatment when there is a perversion in place. The tantalizing environment affords the hope of a satisfaction that can never truly be satisfying and therefore creates a reiterative yearning that can never be relieved.

Winnicott (1963/1989) suggests that the phenomenon he terms fear of breakdown occurs when the individual looks to the present for the event that occurred in the past because there are details that *have not yet been experienced.* Events that are too traumatic to actively endure push us outside of self-experience. They happen as though occurring to another person or else are not encoded into verbal memory at all, but rather remain in the realm of body memories or "dark holes" of unremembered experience. "The original experience of primitive agony cannot get into the past tense unless the ego can first gather it into its own present time experience" (p. 89). For Winnicott, this opportunity presents itself through the transference relationship, through the therapist's failures and mistakes. Eventually, he contends, patient and therapist will come up against their own inevitable failure. If therapist and patient can tolerate this failure, then there is the possibility that the feared event can be experienced in the present. The paradox, of course, is that the event can only be *experienced* because it was never sufficiently encoded to be *remembered,* in the traditional sense of the word. As such, it can only be experienced. The technical issue, then, is to be able to invite an experience that can be used rather than one that will merely be further traumatizing.

The patient needs to "remember" [the breakdown] but it is not possible to remember something that has not yet happened, and this thing of the past has not happened yet because the patient was not there for it to happen to. The only way to "remember" in this case is for the patient to experience this past thing for the first time in the present, that is to say, in the transference. This past and future thing then becomes a matter of the here and now, and becomes experienced by the patient for the first time. This is the equivalent of remembering. (Winnicott, 1963/1989, p. 89)

When individuals have been so severely traumatized that their ego development has been waylaid, they often live their lives terribly constrained, ever vigilant for signs of danger. This vigilance can be so extreme that the person lives her life as though the danger that has already happened is always at imminent risk of occurring. When there has been a perversion in early relationships, as in the case of child sexual abuse, the situation is further complicated by the tantalizing aspects. Furthermore, with trauma, as with most intense emotion, there can be a confusion between past, present, and future that can leave one in an exhausted state of hyperarousal with little relief and little means to engage with others sufficiently to learn something about the conditions under which safety might be distinguished from danger. As Winnicott notes, there is the paradoxical certainty of danger without sufficient recollection of the particulars of that danger to be able to make sense of the experience, integrate it, and work it through. Further complicating these dilemmas is the issue of dependence on unreliable others such that the trauma occurs, not because something happened, but because someone was not there when needed. Childhood trauma often includes, along with abuse, the terrible absence of nothing happening precisely when help was needed

Mary grew up in a household in which parental deprivation and attacks left the children open to boundary violations that took whatever love and care they felt for one another and made those bonds inaccessible as sources of real comfort. Most traumatic had been the sexual abuse that occurred at the hands of her otherwise most "loving" brother. Without care or comfort, Mary was pushed beyond the limits of what she could endure without breakdown. In later years, deeply confused and shamed, without clear recall of some of the most traumatic events of her childhood, Mary found herself isolated and alone, and so frightened of engaging with others that she had found it difficult to build supportive relationships. To the contrary, her relationships often took the form of sadomasochistic engagements that were familiar because they were so similar in affective tone to those from her childhood.

When considering Mary's dilemma, it is useful to have in mind Lacan's (1978) ideas about Lack, Limit, and the importance of the *Third*: the external perspective through which violations can be recognized and affirmed. When parents fail to hold essential boundaries between right and wrong, and between self and other, it becomes very difficult for the child to recognize real limits and thus to be able to attend adaptively to real needs for safety and sustenance. In this case, we will see how Mary became fragmented and virtually unable to *know*, to perceive information that would be vital in making sense of dangers, real and imagined. In our work together, she repeatedly came up against the limits of what she could *usefully* know. Part of our work then, involved my being able to perceive what she could not know but needed to know, to be able to hold this information, and then to enable her to discover a way to encounter it herself without falling into bits. In Bion's terms, as noted in Chapter 7, this confrontation can be seen as an *attack on linking* in which meaning cannot be made from the facts as they are perceived and experienced. In Winnicott's terms, we can see Mary's predicament as an impossible fear of the breakdown that has already occurred.

Mary describes a household in which the father's aggression goes uncontained. There is no maternal or paternal law: no "Third," no external point of reference by which the parents could be judged in relation to their jobs as parents. Without this reference point, Mary was foundering, unable to create a coherent narrative in which living could be seen as worth the fight or to even envision a self worth fighting for. She presents with something that is known and something that is un-known; something missing that might be needed in order to build a life. Mary's mother would tell her that she wished that Mary had never been born, thus offering no maternal affirmation that Mary was even entitled to a life. Similarly, there were no parental injunctions to be relied on, no Law that might have registered the brother's lawlessness and marked his transgressions. There was no parental authority through which to catch him in the act or hold in mind the violation. It is the failure to hold in mind the *fact* of the rupture that makes of it what Lacan (1962–63) calls the "*passage into action*" that retraumatizes, rather than an *enactment* out of which meaning might be made. Bentolila (2007) notes that the passage into action differs from an enactment in that it is *not reversible*. Something has been done that cannot be undone; there is a rupture that cannot so easily be repaired by bringing it into words.

Because the event cannot be held in mind, there is no means for consensual recognition. Perhaps most problematic for Mary, what is missing is the *meaning* of the most problematic events in her past. The brother's violation is often unremembered; recalled merely in fleeting glimpses and fragments that feel so distant that she is not certain of their veracity. Deeper still, perhaps, is the failure pointed to by Winnicott in terms of the mother's willingness to abandon her daughter. Although the mother was ostensibly present, there was no recognition of Mary as a separate and unique subject, entitled to her life, much less fair treatment. In our work together, the absence of benign parental authority as *even a possibility* could be seen, over time, in Mary's aversion of gaze. Even when she would try to make eye contact, her eyes would slip to the side. There was no capacity to actually meet the gaze of the other. Shame was so entrenched that the possibility of encountering a benign other was virtually nonexistent. Something had been broken that resisted repair, in part because Mary could not even be certain that the events at question had actually transpired.

My confusion over what was known or not known between us was complicated by Mary's ambivalent desire to believe that the traumatic events had not transpired but rather that she had just made them up. Our best gauge, then, of the veracity of Mary's recollections were the "memories in feeling" (Klein, 1957), the "language of the body" (Charles, 2002b) through which Mary marked the distress that at times was inaccessible or inadmissible to her conscious mind. Her hold on the reality of her traumatic experiences was so precarious that, as she moved towards voicing her experience to another person, the annihilation anxiety was almost unbearable.

This was the context in which Mary came to see me. Initially, she was like a frightened rabbit, ready to run. Over time, however, she slowly began to be able to be more present and struggled more actively with what she could see as her own self-destructiveness. Rather than feeling entirely like a victim, she was beginning to recognize ways in which she was complicit in allowing others to destroy her. This recognition afforded the terrible realization that, if she truly wanted to have a life, she would have to come to the fore as an active agent and recognize her own potency. Such a move would entail integrating good and bad aspects of self and other. During this time, Mary reported a dream in which she was encircled by barbed wire in an empty room. She was trying to chew her way out but not having much success. Very vivid for me, as she reported this dream, was my sense of her alliance with the pain such that her main enemy seemed to be her love of the pain. Processing this dream helped Mary to recognize that the sadomasochism prevalent in her most intimate relationships was patterned after her relationship with her mother. Recognizing her own part in these interactions left her feeling shaken and raw.

It was in this context that Mary began to notice and explicitly bring into our work some of the gaps she encountered. On one occasion, for example, she spoke of her puzzlement over an experience in which she could see her own ability to elide from consciousness information that was so troubling that, while evident to others, it remained entirely obscure to her. She told me about an event that had occurred over the weekend, in which she had recognized that she had been missing meanings that seemed obvious to others. She was ashamed but also curious as to the possible meanings of this gap she had encountered. She talked about playing the game charades with friends, and finding herself unable to put together meanings that seemed to be apparent to everyone else.

"We were playing charades and the word was 'blow' and the guy decided to get to 'blow' by using the word 'blow-job.' He said something about 'sexual perversion' and then 'jobs' and I'm thinking 'jobs . . . sexual perversion . . . what the hell is this?' and I'm just not getting it. And everyone is laughing and laughing. And I just couldn't get it. Was my face red."

She then told me that she had been listening to a song and felt as though she finally heard the words as though for the first time. She repeated the lyrics: "'boy, you best pray that I bleed real soon—how's that thought for you?'" and then said "and I finally get it and I think, 'God, how stupid.'" I was struck, in the moment, by my recognition that she had always thought that the lyrics had referred to cutting and that she now could see that they related to pregnancy. When I asked her why she felt stupid, she replied, "Just not wanting to think about pregnancy or any of that. Just not getting it."

I was struck by her view of herself as stupid in relation to not understanding, and wondered aloud about the origins of this view. "It's interesting that you would decide that you're stupid. We all miss things. I'm thinking that, with the first example, with everyone laughing, it makes sense that you would feel stupid but with the second example, you were alone, up against your internal critic. I'm wondering where that came from; wondering about when you were young—your experience of feeling laughed at or ridiculed or criticized."

"Oh that," she responded, with a wry look of acknowledgment on her face. "There was certainly a lot of that." Suddenly, a wave hit and her face became dark with distress. She curled up in a ball in her chair.

"What?" I asked.

"I feel like I just went down a rabbit hole," she replied.

I found myself thinking 'blow-job,' 'blood,' 'brother,' and wondered how much I could say of what was in my mind. After a bit of time, I remarked tentatively that I was thinking of where the session had begun. She nodded but said nothing. After more time had passed, I asked her how she was doing. She described her pain in bullet points: "intensity; noise; voices."

Then, "I don't know if I can do this," she said.

"I don't know if you can afford not to," I replied.

Over several sessions, we worked to process this experience. Recognizing the elements that had been elided from consciousness forced Mary into an encounter with an all too present past, through which she was faced with the abuse that she most often consciously denied. This was an almost intolerable experience for us both and she came upon the awareness slowly and with resistance. "I'm trying to avoid climbing into a bottle or cutting myself," she reported at the beginning of one hour. "Sleep seemed to be the best option. I just can't figure out what's going on. I keep going over and over it and I just can't get it. I feel like I keep missing something."

I asked her how she put it together. "I came in, talking about not being able to put things together," she said, "then I started thinking about childhood and all the things I couldn't make sense of, and they just kept marching across, the whole progression. And then this pain, and this wailing, and 'stop it' and 'don't do that!' and I just can't make sense of it."

"It seems to have something to do with 'blow-job' and 'blood' and not being able to stop it or get anyone to help," I said.

"I just can't tell what's true and what's not. I spent so much time convincing myself it wasn't true and most of my adult life putting it to rest. I just can't even tell what's true." She paused, then mused, "It seems like a story I told myself."

"*That* may be the story you tell yourself to lull yourself," I replied.

"Seems like a dream."

"A dream you dream to avoid the nightmare?" I persisted.

At this point, Mary was curled up tightly into a ball in her chair, and I was aware that our conversation had turned into a sadomasochistic enactment in which I was persecuting her through my persistence. At that point, I too felt confused regarding what might or could be known between us. I tried to join her. "Tell me about the nightmare," I said, and she smiled, apparently grateful for this offering of a bit of respite from what had seemed like too terrible a reality to encounter. This displacement seemed to enable us to work together.

"It's very dark," she began. "I'm very small—and I'm scared—and in pain." When I asked where she hurt, she surprised me by responding, "My heart, my soul—it's like broken. I'm broken." After a long, terrible pause that I found almost unendurable, buffeted by my desire that she not be broken and my utter powerlessness in the face of her feelings, she said, "I wish I was dead." These words cut the silence with raw emotion, like a knife blade. My thoughts were full of memories of Mary's descriptions of her mother's wish that Mary had never been born and Mary's ritualized repetitive enactment of this wish through her cutting.

I tried to put some distance between the past and the present: "That was certainly the message you got. Hard to know how to survive that then." This time, I was the one who had a song running through my head, and I repeated the lyrics aloud to her: "Hold on—hold on to yourself—this is gonna hurt like hell." She smiled in recognition, and this moment seemed to help her to mobilize her present self and to face the end of the hour with a wry smile.

The hours that followed were difficult ones. At times, Mary was her adult self, and we could put together pieces from past and present. At other moments, she seemed immobilized, and her voice emerged like a tiny and terrible whispered scream. "Don't," she said. "No, no, don't." In such moments, I could see that remembering the abuse at the hands of her brother was like reliving it. She struggled to stay present with the experience and to also try to speak to me about it, but at times it was virtually impossible.

At one point, she said "I can't go there."

And, with Winnicott in mind, I replied, "It's there. It's already happened. Not knowing it just keeps you from being able to move on."

"I don't even know if it's true," she replied, after a silence.

"You know what you feel," I replied. "He betrayed you. And then you betrayed yourself by pretending. That's how you survived. But now it's killing you." After another pause, I said, "It's hard because you can't afford to force yourself, because that's part of the problem." And then later, in the same hour, I went on, "You're on a tightrope and the important thing is to find your balance at any given moment—to take care of yourself—to keep yourself as the frame of reference and not get lost."

In this last statement, we can see my awareness of the importance of attending to her subjectivity even before I had Lacan's conceptualizations explicitly in mind. When we look at such clinical moments, we can see that it is the necessity that drives the intervention and the theory. The theory merely affords a way of organizing those understandings. That moment was a turning point in the treatment. Locating the breakdown in the past and the survival in the present helped Mary to be able to recognize both her surrender and her survival.

What we were left with, then, was the challenge of how we could help her to become less frozen in the past, to afford her sufficient perspective that we might be able to reclaim those aspects of herself that had been left behind when she was forced beyond her ability to tolerate or integrate her experience, and then left with insufficient parental attention to recognize the trauma in ways that might have protected her and helped her to heal. Perhaps most fundamentally, what had been missing was the type of parental attention that should have recognized and affirmed the essential importance of Mary as an independent subject in need of care, support, and respect.

The child who fails to find herself in the gleam in her parent's eyes is a lost soul. This child can spend her life looking in all the wrong places for that gleam she sensed she needed, even though she may have lost touch with any idea of what is being sought. The deficit, then, is experienced as a painful absence that cannot be relieved. Because the gleam is linked with the parents, we can spend our lives seeking out exactly the types of disappointments that are all too familiar. Without an understanding of what impels us, we can assign blame to the seeker by using labels such as "self-defeating," "self-destructive," and "masochistic," each of which describes the resulting behavior without recognizing the underlying source. These types of labels tend to further entrench the self-blame rather than illuminating the underlying dynamic.

The passage into action can be a useful concept in such cases because it highlights the fact of a rupture that has occurred and must be taken into account. There are barriers that are never meant to be broken that, once ruptured, cannot truly be repaired. Recognizing this fact can provide relief to the person who finds herself on the other side of the looking glass, gazing back longingly at the life she might have hoped to have lived but that has been sealed off forever. Mourning such a loss requires great courage and fortitude, facilitated by the respectful recognition of a therapist who does not minimize the rupture but who also believes that it can be survived, that life can be better than it has been.

Mary was fundamentally changed by this work that we did together. No longer so powerfully persecuted by others, she began to locate herself as an active agent in her life. Increasingly, our hours were filled, not with the deadly and dark silence of primitive agonies, but rather with Mary's descriptions of insights attained and challenges met. She began to be able to spend more time in interaction with others. Not only was she able to enjoy these encounters, she was also increasingly able to keep her eyes open and meet the gaze of the other. Over time, Mary learned to locate deficits and strengths in herself and in others, and to navigate accordingly. Critical to these changes was, first, Mary's ability to recognize the passage into action from the past—the point at which she was thrust beyond endurance and could not sustain her own ego integrity—and, second, our ability to encounter the past in the present and sustain our engagement with one another. Only in this way were we able to work together to integrate the disparate pieces of unlinked fragments and build a narrative that was both survivable and sufficiently in touch with reality constraints to be able to move forward past the point at which the development had been impeded.

Chapter Nine

Telling Trauma

Part I: Working with Psychosis

Working with psychotic experience poses particular challenges for clinicians, calling on us to get in touch with psychotic aspects of our own personalities while also keeping our anchors in consensual reality. In a society in which psychosis is increasingly seen as a function of physiological anomaly and pathology, it can be difficult for the psychoanalytic psychotherapist to maintain a respectful working relationship with the person designated "psychotic." In this chapter I will discuss my work with an individual whose experience of "losing her mind" invited me to move into a space in which I might also lose *my* mind (thus endorsing the hope that one can lose one's mind and re-find it). In spite of theories that warn of the perils of fragmentation and splitting, we are tempted to decline the patient's invitation, designating the patient as a devalued Other to deny our own vulnerability. Joining together in our refusal to turn a blind eye on our common humanity helps support the difficult work with patients who demand entry into that shaky but essential territory of the unknown.

Amended version of a paper presented at the ISPS-US Ninth Annual Meeting, New York City, March 15, 2008.

We find ourselves at an odd point in history where our understanding of what "works" in therapy may be in stark contrast to ideas regarding "best practice." And yet, if we are to work respectfully with individuals who at times move into psychotic territories, we are going to have to *first* be willing to lose our minds sufficiently to have a sense of what our patients are up against and *then* be able to recover sufficiently to be able to have anything of value to offer.

The psychodynamic clinician assumes that problems are best understood in the context of the life narrative in which they are embedded, and yet current standards of care define and prescribe ways of viewing patients and attending to their distress that may be too simplistic to facilitate the type of individual development we hope to invite. In this chapter, I offer a plea for a measure of abnormality (see McDougall, 1980) and also for a measure of respect for the individual who is struggling with experience that not only goes beyond the social norms but is also seen as something to eradicate in the current cultural context. Contrary to other cultures in which paranormal experience has been highly valued, in Western culture we are wary of any experience or behavior that strays too far from social norms and conventions. As a result, those who have been so traumatized that they have been pushed beyond their ability to stay within those social conventions are often further traumatized by the ways in which they are treated. Their isolation then further exacerbates their distress.

I have discussed previously the difficulties psychoanalytic practitioners face in an era of managed care and simplistically defined "evidence" (Charles, 2008, 2009). In this chapter, I will merely affirm the importance of maintaining humanity as a core value lest we be drawn, as McWilliams puts it, into efforts to "medicate, manage, reeducate, control, and correct the irrational behavior of people whose suffering is inconvenient to the larger culture" (2005, p. 140). If we are mindful of how attempts to manage behavior may not only be dehumanizing, but may also interfere with *self-management*, we can see how the therapist's move to a managerial position can invite opposition or compliance rather than more adaptive reflective understanding.

The press towards simplistic models is particularly problematic for those whose more complex symptom pictures offer no easy match between problem and solution (Westen, Novotny, & Thompson-Brenner, 2004; Charles, 2011). In some ways, being seen as a problem to be solved may further complicate an individual's attempt towards recovery, particularly when the traumatic story being told through the symptom is obscured by the very diagnosis that attempts to describe where the trouble lies (Andreason, 2007; Morgan & Fisher, 2007). Although diagnoses can help us to hold in mind constellations of symptoms in useful ways, there is also a tendency to reify diagnoses such that the context—and, with it, the meanings—can disappear. Our respectful interest in trying to understand the contexts in which the individual's life has been disrupted importantly affirms that meaning *can* be made. This translation process requires sufficient mental space for reflection, in Lacan's terms, "the Third": a triadic structure that grounds the therapeutic dyad within a system of rules (Muller, 2007). For Lacan (1977c, 1993), the primary difficulty in working with psychosis is the tendency for the psychotic individual to locate meanings outside of consensual reality, such that there is no third perspective possible and therefore no way to locate meanings in relation to one another.

Although the current trend towards evidence-based practice represents an appeal to just such a Third, this trend can also undermine our need, as professionals, to remain in active dialogue with whatever standards are in place. Our ethical codes often do not dictate a clear path (Knapp, Berman, Gottlieb, & Handelsman, 2007), as, for example, when the principles of beneficence and nonmalfeasance are at odds with respect for patient autonomy (Knapp & Vandecreek, 2007). When working with very disturbed patients, it may be easy to move towards believing that beneficence has greater value than respect for patient autonomy and yet this type of move may endanger that individual's relatively fragile autonomy and ego integrity, confusing humanism with paternalism.

A respectful humanism may be particularly important in our work with traumatized individuals, who can become increasingly dysregulated and disorganized when the interpretations and demands of those who would ostensibly provide "care" fail to respect the other's perspective. Complicating these interactions is how very difficult it can be to work with such an individual without becoming increasingly dysregulated oneself. Thus one can well understand the impetus of caregivers to medicate symptoms or manage behaviors so as to de-escalate the level of distress. I will offer some reflections on my work with one such patient, by way of affirming some of the difficulties and some of the potential in maintaining one's determination to lodge one's theory in a language of *trauma* rather than *psychopathology*.

This work is facilitated by ideas culled from authors who have used ideas from Bion and Lacan to point to the importance of listening for the story that is being told through the symptom (Apollon, Bergeron, & Cantin, 2002; Bion, 1967a; Davoine & Gaudillière, 2004). These authors note the particular qualities of the traumatic story that may be told, in part, through the ellipses: through what is missing (Lacan, 1977d). When part of what is missing is coherence—the narrative element that holds the story together—the listener is then left with gaps that designate that which has been left unrepresented and seems unrepresentable (Charles, 2006b). Meeting the person who cannot meet him- or herself is a difficult task that occurs slowly and painstakingly over time. Through our persistence, we make the statement that that person is worth discovering, on her own terms, in her own right (Charles, 2004b). In this way, we hope to invite the other's interest in self sufficiently that we might work together in the painstaking and often painful process of discovering what lies beyond the gap.

Christine initially presented as a stiff and seemingly brittle young woman with a wide-eyed stare but little sense of actual engagement. She appeared, in her hair and dress, to have emerged from the 1950's. She was polite but remote, speaking so softly that she was difficult to hear. Her speech was abstract and ruminative, making it difficult for the listener to join her in conversation or even follow the thread. She seemed caught by despair over what had been lost and was now out of reach, unable to locate any hope, desire, or volition, telling a story about losing something that could never be re-found. The listener was left to imagine the details or even how this story might fit into a coherent narrative.

Christine found it exceptionally difficult to settle into treatment and seemed to be leaving before she had even arrived. Initially, her distress split between being offered a woman therapist rather than a man versus getting out of Austen Riggs entirely. She recurrently expressed her determination to "get things in place" so that she could "move forward" in her life or "move towards health"; statements that remained abstract with no clear referents such that they became increasingly meaningless to me. Alternatively, she referred to an equally inchoate series of "unfortunate events" that had landed her in her current state, which she intended to remediate with due expediency. Throughout her time at the Center, Christine seemed actively engaged in trying to leave, while feeling as though she was becoming further mired in her distress, in a highly dangerous, but tantalizing, environment. Her terror colored the landscape with shock waves of her own distress. I felt as though there was an oddly restrained tempest passing daily through my office, pausing briefly but never entirely settling in place, and I longed to make contact with the person beyond the chaos.

Trying to talk to Christine was difficult, as she seemed to be ruled by ideas of politeness that insisted, for example, on my not interrupting. I found myself faced with a barrage of words that might halt midstream, as she sat, reflecting raptly before resuming. She would then gear up again towards the end of that sentence and rush precipitously without pause into the next thought. Once firmly embedded in that statement, she could once again pause for air and the series would repeat itself. She was rigidly polite when I interrupted, either ignoring my rudeness and continuing on her way with a fixed, tight smile, or stopping and staring through me while waiting for me to finish. Nothing I said seemed quite right and attempts to locate her were invariably and inevitably wrong. Clarification, however, was rarely forthcoming. She was just as elusive in terms of locating any facts on which we might land together as she was in developing a dialogue in which two people might actively engage.

We did seem to be able to agree that an unfortunate series of events had landed her, not only at Riggs, but also in my office. The latter was included under the rubric not only of "unfortunate events" but also of institutional inadequacy. We were victims of an unfortunate system that had paired us together, leaving us to attempt to find our way dutifully through the ensuing mess.

Christine's talk during sessions often began with laments about whatever it had been that had derailed her, events that seemed quite vivid in her mind but which she described stringently and abstractly. Statements such as "well, of course, if 'it' hadn't happened" or "of course I just couldn't possibly" or "moving towards health" came to seem like coded phrases that obstructed her from view while also providing clues regarding possible meanings in her narrative. Her stories were tempered by graciously expressed anecdotes of having her best efforts waylaid by the incompetence of staff who couldn't manage things properly, and her affect ranged from indulgence to outrage to despair.

Initially, I found myself trying and failing to locate her needs, thoughts, feelings, and desires sufficiently to be able to have any point of contact, while feeling as though she was a storm passing through my office on her way back either to outpatient treatment or to a male therapist. Often, I wished she *would* just finally pass through. Over time, however, she did not leave and she did seem to register my attempts to understand her from her perspective. This recognition formed a tenuous alliance through which she began to tell me more directly about her distress rather than talking *at* me with no feeling of actual engagement.

During this time, Christine seemed to use me as a touchstone with whom to touch base when she was feeling particularly lost. It was not uncommon to find her in the hall or stairway, waiting for me to walk by, or standing quietly outside my office door, silently waiting for me to look up and notice her. At these times, she would apologetically relate a concern or request a bit of information. Rarely did she take up more than a minute or two of time. Rather, she seemed to be using me as an orienting point of human contact. She felt like a tragic figure, haunting the halls.

Periodic family meetings were useful in helping me to understand some of Christine's dilemmas in her family. Her intent to leave treatment because of financial strains had been incomprehensible in light of the parents' stated intention to support her treatment. However, the family conversation soon revealed that no one actually intended to offer financial support, and what had seemed to be a likely plan—conserving resources while living with her mother—began to sound quite deadly. I could hear how each family member overrode her, offering untenable resolutions to her dilemma. Much as I had found when trying to take the life history, Christine seemed to exist as an unwieldy, relatively undefined object in the mind of each family member, with no real agreement amongst any dyad as to what the trouble might be.

Their trauma over having already lost one child to suicide seemed to make it difficult for them to express concern with sufficient emotional distance to leave any room for reflection.

At that point, I could register from my own experience what had seemed too abstract, ill-defined, or remote to have been recognizable previously. Christine and I began to have more meeting points, and she continued to become increasingly calm, which further aided our ability to engage. She had always alluded to having "lost her mind," and needing to be very careful not to do so again, and now I could see that she had relatively clear, experience-based ideas regarding what she did and did not need, and what was and was not good for her. Through this new lens, I could not only see her desperately fighting her way back to greater equilibrium, I could also understand what she had been trying to tell me about how threatening the disequilibrium had been after her sibling's suicide.

Through this greater understanding, it became easier to have a sense of Christine's needs, capacities, and resources, and to begin to build a plan together that made sense and seemed viable. She began to mark a need for what I called "home," but we were also able to understand why my use of that word was so problematic for her, home having been absolutely not safe. We began to define "home" in *her* terms: having some of her good friends nearby and a therapist on whom she can rely. Perhaps most important to Christine was her longing for a job, which had been so integral to her sense of identity, security, and self-worth. We began to build a discharge plan that took these needs into account, while also leaving room for her considerable ambivalence.

Before the case conference that marked the end of the initial treatment and evaluation period at the hospital, I had heard from the nursing staff that Christine was not planning to attend. The interview with the patient at the case conference is an important moment that enables the staff to hear what is most pressing for the patient, from her own perspective. I encouraged Christine to think about what she might like to say to us, stressing the importance of our hearing in her own voice what she would like us to help her with; that in the absence of her voice to guide us, we would have our own ideas about being helpful that might be just as well-intentioned and just as unhelpful as her family's suggestions. This advice seemed to make sense to her.

What enabled me to encourage Christine to face us was my conviction that I have colleagues who can hear the voice of traumatic memory with respect, without turning away; who can tolerate sounding within themselves those terrible notes that can tie us intolerably close together, as we sit with those who feel as though they have lost their minds. I don't think we can manage to sit with such patients constructively without being willing to confront the possibility of losing our own minds, as they invite us dangerously into the terrible spaces in which they are lost; these collapsed universes of fragmented, ominous meanings, with no help at hand. This willingness to find within ourselves whatever we might most resist is, I think, a precondition for respectful work with deeply troubled individuals (see, for example, Bion, 1967a; Charles, 2004a). Accordingly, part of the work entails being willing to be untethered and unhelpful; to tolerate our own failure in relation to the disaster that has already happened (Winnicott, 1963/1989) so that we might accept together whatever need be accepted so that we might find our way back, together.

Coming to the case conference provided an important opportunity for Christine to confront her fears of being un- or mis-recognized. Having felt so demeaned by her suffering and her inability to hold on to the things she held most dear, her shame had kept her virtually hidden from view, frightened of articulating a need, much less a desire. Taking the risk of speaking enabled her to see that she could be taken seriously, a precarious position for her, so certain was she of her utter worthlessness. The subsequent family meeting provided further ballast, as we worked to distinguish her parents' fears from their love and concern. Clarifying this distinction helped Christine to recognize ways in which their anxiety subverts their care and undermines their supportive intentions. She could see that what she experiences as a lack of faith in her competence is actually a function of their anxiety. This insight helped her to think about how she might accept their care without entirely losing sight of her strengths, as she continued to try to figure out how to move forward in her life.

Christine seemed to stabilize after the family meeting. Particularly useful to her was having noted my ability to mark her struggles *and* her successes. This recognition helped her to mobilize her own efforts, and she began to talk about never having left room for pleasure in her life. This desire opened up a space for constructive thought and action, which unfortunately was then derailed by her mother's anxiety, precipitating an abrupt rise in Christine's distress and disorganization. It took several weeks to begin to recover from this event, and she was not able to achieve that higher level of organization during her remaining time at the Center. She *was* able, however, to talk about the difficulties she faces in loving her parents and wanting their support, the guilt she feels for failing to support *them*, and the terrible price of too much contact.

I put forward this case because Christine was so difficult to engage with that she raised the discomfort of those working with her to intolerable levels. This discomfort invited others to respond to her as though she was hopelessly psychotic or characterologically borderline rather than functioning at a borderline level of ego integration that threatened to slip into psychotic regions. As such, her efforts towards competence tended to invite opposition rather than support, further increasing her isolation, despair, and disorganization. At that point, it was easy to see her as psychotic in a way that demands medication rather than as traumatically disorganized in a way that invites respect, care, and understanding.

Working in a system where each professional guild—social work, psychology, psychiatry—has a different lens through which symptoms and treatment might be viewed, one of my tasks had been to try to avoid the type of adversarial relations in which meaning can be lost as complex realities are split into dichotomous either-or dilemmas. In such circumstances, projections are easily taken as data and offered up as facts that further mobilize the anxiety driving the projections. It is then easy to find oneself lodged into entrenched "us" versus "them" dichotomies, feeling as though we are fighting for something urgently important without being able to reflectively consider the positions being endorsed or opposed, much less unpack their various meanings within the system. As Matte-Blanco (1975) notes, at a certain level, affective intensity can preclude reflective thought and certainty can become rigid, unyielding, and destructive.

How, then, do we grapple with the dilemma described by Bion (1977), in which whatever idea dysregulates the system is inevitably opposed but is also *needed* for growth to occur, making it important for group members to speak to aspects of conscience that have *not* been voiced. Although we may find the anxiety and uncertainty that accompany moral distress aversive, these experiences may be fundamental to ethical behavior. As Bauman (1993) puts it: "The moral self is a self always haunted by the suspicion that it is not moral enough" (p. 80).

At Austen Riggs, we have the complicated advantage of being part of a therapeutic community, which helps us to recognize how complicated it can be for an individual to become part of the social matrix. For individuals who struggle with psychosis, the dilemma of inclusion is particularly problematic. The psychotic individual often sees too much and has insufficiently internalized the barriers of social convention. Her comments, then, can be virtually unassimilable in the social matrix, perhaps most particularly when they are spot-on. At Riggs, we are advised to "always think about how the other person is right" (Shapiro & Carr, 1991), but it can be extremely difficult to listen from this perspective. Trying to see from the other's perspective, however, can help take us out of the pressurized polarizations that arise so that we might think more deeply about those ideas that most invite our resistance.

My sensitivity to the "outsider" position (Charles, 2001a, b, 2004b; Charles & Telis, 2009), and to the traumatic effects when "difference" leads to devaluation (Charles, 2001c) perhaps increases my awareness that my difficulties in joining this complex system parallel the difficulties patients encounter in their own entries. This resonance is colored by my experience of being a woman in a culture in which history has been written by men, and by my struggles to find my own voice without being silenced or becoming stridently reactive. My own struggles to locate my voice as part of a symphony of disparate voices in this complicated community have added to my empathic resonance to my patients, who are grappling with this complexity from their own perspectives. This resonance becomes part of the translation process, as we utilize theory and personal and clinical experience in the service of the patient's development. We also recognize the *price* of learning from another, which helps us perhaps step back a bit, as Winnicott (1971) suggests, and not spoil our patients' discoveries by insisting on articulating what they are coming to know through their own experience. Knowledge gained through the lived moment tends to be more accessible and adaptable than received knowledge.

In addition, being able to come to this type of understanding oneself helps to build self-respect and self-reliance, making it easier to tolerate difference and work through difficulties as they arise. This ability to tolerate and respect difference is particularly important for the therapist, who is faced continually with seemingly disparate experiences. When we are able to share difficulties rather than feeling persecuted by the Other, we manage much better. As we become polarized, it is important to remind ourselves of our common goals and our respective challenges. Without hearing back from the other, it is easy to fall back into the model mentioned earlier in which the intent to give care can invite opposition to being "treated" in ways that are dehumanizing. Although dichotomous categories help us to anchor understanding and to demarcate self and other, they are inevitably simplistic. Whether we are talking in terms of cultural delineations, diagnostic labels, or theoretical dogma, our demarcations can close down conversation rather than open dialogue, as apparent sameness obscures difference, and apparent difference obscures similarities of meaning, each inhibiting new learning.

As the patient's voice, will, and authority drop out of the conversation, it becomes increasingly difficult for the "care provider" to have any real sense of what providing care means or of the price exacted through that process. One of my patients introduced me to the word "civility," as described by Shils (1997). This word beautifully captures an issue that is pivotal in our attempts to work with one another. As we fight for the salience of our own perspective over others, it is easy to forget this principle of "civility"; to fail to listen sufficiently respectfully to the other to see what they or we might be missing that might add to our shared understanding. If, on the other hand, we take this principle seriously, we are in a better position to invite the best from others, rather than inviting reactivity, resentment, and resistance. A simple principle, perhaps, but one that we could all benefit from heeding more carefully.

That patient also offered me a quote from Unamuno (1921), which seems an apt way to close: "Warmth, warmth, more warmth! for we are dying of cold and not of darkness. It is not the night that kills, but the frost" (Miguel de Unamuno).

Chapter Ten

Telling Trauma

Part II: Signs, Symbols, and Symptoms

Working with traumatized individuals is particularly complicated because trauma itself disrupts the signification processes so essential to the integration or narration of a coherent story. The story is then told through symptoms that we register *implicitly* through the sensory registers of the less conscious mind. Although we talk in theory about unconscious processes, in practice it is easy to discount this information and to fail to develop our capacities to utilize it. In our rational, pragmatic society, it may be the attachment literature that best helps us see how competently our sensory registers function; how much information we take in from tone, gesture, and even smell. The smell of fear is unmistakable, even when the person is covering their terror in other ways. In the face of such terror, it is easy to resist believing that "there but for the grace of God, go I"; to resist knowing that we, too, might be so terribly devastated by encounters with life's adversities. We have developed ways of fending off the common thread that might tie us too uncomfortably to the severely traumatized individual. In this act, however, we further sever a crucial thread tying that individual to the social matrix, and run the risk of pushing that person further outside the range of the common human discourse. In this way, we create an alienated Other, who then represents not only his or her personal narrative, but also the narrative of exclusion in which we have become implicated. The story is then told in other registers through the symptoms. In such cases, the symptoms can be seen as signifiers that fall outside the realm of consensual Language. These signifiers are often quite concrete, as we will see in the case example, signs that mark meanings that are not yet clearly elaborated into symbols. These signs may be viewed from a Kleinian perspective as *symbolic equations*. Through the case example, we can consider ways in which the young woman who cannot tell her story directly might be speaking to us through her symptoms.

Amended version of a paper presented at the ISPS International Congress, Copenhagen, Denmark, June 16, 2009, and at APA 2009, Toronto, August 8, 2009.

We rely on our patients to tell us a story that makes sense enough that we can locate the points of tension. As noted previously, however, for individuals whose lives have been severely disrupted, it is often the gap that marks meaning in a story that is told and untold at the same time. For the therapist, it is our attunement that enables us to come into resonance with another person sufficiently to enable us to register what is absent as well as what is present. In this process, we also learn to appreciate the enormity of the challenge. When working with psychosis, in particular, there is always the risk that we won't be able to tolerate being submerged in these strange waters, and so will pull away, gasping for breath, and anchor ourselves in the firmer ground of diagnoses, medications, and treatment plans that can be marked and managed over time, rather than allowing time to reassert itself as the narrative emerges.

I grew up in the era of *I Never Promised You a Rose Garden* (Greenberg, 1964) and Fire and Rain (Taylor, 1970), a time when young Americans were struggling to make sense of trauma that seemed to impinge from such a distance that it could not be easily integrated. The romantic notions of psychosis prevalent at that time may have skewed my thinking away from its more tragic aspects, but also lodged in me a deep respect for the human suffering thus marked. Several generations later, we are deluged with data about the atrocities we inflict on one another but seem no closer to integrating these bits into a worldview that is both safe and human; to look inward at our own inhumanity rather than splitting it off into the other.

Psychosis often emerges during the adolescent passage. The task of defining oneself as a separate autonomous being is complicated when trauma has impeded that process in previous generations. Americans carry the complicated legacy of a hopeful belief that one might somehow move forward unfettered by complications of individual or socio-cultural difference. From this framework, difference itself is dissociated, not only dislocating us from the cultural traditions that aid mourning (Akhtar, 1995; Apprey, 1993; Charles, 2000), but also obscuring the type of structural trauma (LaCapra, 1999) that marks a defect in the social fabric.

The psychotic stands outside consensual discourse, commenting from the side, like a Greek chorus. In contrast to the medical model of psychosis seen in terms of aberrant signals, psychodynamic clinicians (e.g., Bion, 1967a) try to understand the frame of reference of the psychotic patient. In a dangerous world, where potential caregivers may not be listening respectfully enough to be worthy of trust in spite of their best intentions, these signals may be seen as necessary distortions in a history that has become unspeakable (Davoine & Gaudillière, 2004). Meaning, then, is organized irrationally, through the nonverbal system of order and rhythm described by Kristeva (1986) as the chora.

For therapists, learning to find our way through the various verbal and nonverbal signals can be disorienting and disorganizing, likely parallel to the very difficulties the patient finds herself in. This is a crucial juncture. If we believe in the importance of an objective order that overrides any individual's subjective experience, this belief leads us to try to help the patient to come in line with that order. If, however, we believe in the validity of individual experience in relation to the social order, we can try to help people think about how to perhaps more adaptively be themselves in the world as it exists and also, perhaps, to think about how to effect useful changes in their social environment.

In doing battle with madness as something to be exorcized or eradicated, *we* become part of a crazy system in which subjective reality is denied. From where, then, might such an individual speak? In organizations that offer a therapeutic milieu as part of the treatment process, one can see that it is often the psychotic who speaks most clearly and directly, nailing whatever dynamic is at play with uncanny acuity. We then see the rush to exorcise that voice from the room, to designate the person "crazy" who dares to speak such difficult truths.

So, then, not only does trauma fragment history, destroying speech and leaving the subject estranged from self and other (Charles, 2005), it also invites our resistance, making it even more difficult for the communication to register and be recognized. In our medicalized world, the very label "psychotic" tends to invite disrespect for the person's capacity to know herself sufficiently to take an active part in her own treatment (Charles, 2008). Language is a consensual act that helps to bridge our isolation from one another. In my own research looking at the narratives of people who have been labeled psychotic, we see how easily meaning can be lost when there is insufficient respect to be able to find it (Charles, Clemence, Newman, & O' Loughlin, 2009). We can all think of times when we found ourselves losing our own point as we tried to explain something to someone who was not understanding. Close observation of interviews shows how an individual who initially seems incoherent can be pulled into coherence by a respectful interviewer who can see beyond the halting speech that is, in part, a function of the expectation of being misunderstood or devalued (Charles, October 9, 2009).

In spite of evidence to the contrary, psychosis tends to be equated with a lack of insight (Amador, Strauss, Yale, Flaum, & Gorman, 1993), so that psychotherapy is framed, not in terms of understanding or accommodating to painful realities, but rather in terms of diagnosing psychopathology and managing problematic behavior. Our idealization of science obscures humanistic values (Peterson, 2004), reinforcing the stigma that impedes long-term recovery (Lysaker, Roe, & Yanos, 2007; Ritsher & Phelan, 2004), and furthering the misrecognition at the crux of the dilemma. Joanne Greenberg (personal communication), author of the fictionalized account of her own psychoanalytic treatment with Frieda Fromm-Reichmann—the famed *I Never Promised You a Rose Garden*—notes that crucial to her own recovery from psychosis was the respectful engagement offered to her by her therapist and some staff members at Chestnut Lodge. This human connection may be *the crucial* lynchpin of any effective treatment (Charles, 2009).

If we adhere to a trauma driven model of psychosis, we find ourselves working outside the realm of history, allowing the trauma to make itself known *as it reverberates* (Caruth, 1991) in the echoes that link us back into the realm of historical time (Davoine & Gaudillière, 2004; Lacan, 1972–1973). Much like Bion's (1967b) admonition to eschew memory or desire, setting aside our preconceptions helps us provide a space in which meaning *might* be made and, perhaps, to tolerate experiencing a world in which thinking—in the sense of linking thoughts logically with one another—is not possible (Lacan, 1978; Bion, 1992). In this pre-symbolic realm of primary process, the psychotic element in *us* is *called forth and resisted* in each encounter, pulling us towards the limits of what we can and cannot manage without feeling at risk of imminent collapse and fragmentation (Bion, 1967a).

It is through our ability to use these experiences as a template that the translation is made. As we begin to find words, we bridge the absolute chasm of otherness, moving from the *symbolic equation*, in which words are *things* rather than representations, towards *symbolization*, using words in a process of exchange, directly and consciously communicating so that meanings can be held, shared, and explored (Segal, 1957). When metaphor has been lost behind the dire pressure to survive, there is often a gap, as I will describe in my work with Leah, between what happens in the body or the mind, and what can be articulated in language.

One of the dilemmas, then, in working with severely traumatized individuals, is this issue of the concreteness of language, where it is not useful as metaphor. There is no space to play with words. It can be difficult for us as clinicians to find our way in such a universe, and yet, this is exactly the challenge being posed. So, for example, we can think of the case of a young woman who has struggled with periods of psychosis to the extent that she at times had little contact with objective reality. At worst, she found herself lost in an alien universe, running from the bar codes that she felt were hounding her. In such a universe, there is no peace, no solace, and no rest.

In the absence of finding another person who might be willing to listen to her story and wonder, along with her, how she had come to be in such a position, it is difficult for Leah to find a place to land. When I met her, she seemed to be caught in an impossible and relentless struggle to repair her "movements" so that she could leave behind the "disarray" and finally become the person she longs to be. In Leah's world, the dividing line between consensual and idiosyncratic reality is not clear, and her observations range from uncannily acute—as when she describes the denied hostility underlying her mother's "good intentions"—to utterly mad, as when she describes with amazement how her father was able to project his face onto a movie screen and speak to her from there. Even now, she is amazed, not at the capacity of her mind to produce such an experience, but by her father's uncanny ability to perform such a feat!

When anxious, Leah easily becomes derailed, whether by a chance movement that startles, or by her internal anxiety at the imminence of impossible meanings. During psychological testing, for example, she was asked to detail the blot elements she had used in a particular percept. When asked "what made it look like a bug?" her demeanor deadened and she responded, "Not really. Um . . . I don't know. I get overstimulated really easily—I react to people's movements. Five, six, seven, eight. I'll say it bluntly because it needs to be said. Six and one-third, five and a half, seven-fifty, eight point six, four point four. Thirty-six to fifty-two, sixteen to ten kind of split. It's all in the second movement and centered . . . "

In our sessions, we can be speaking about the most mundane matters and then veer suddenly into territory inhabited by the magical numbers, colors, and sequences that organize her universe, accompanied by the cacophony of the voices that may seem to come from benign and helpful gods or may turn mischievous and betray her by pretending, for example, to be the voice of her dead grandmother, eventually betraying themselves through the emptiness and vacuity of their routinized phrases.

References to numbers as powerful signs came up early in our work, as she told me about the behavioral outbursts that were threatening her treatment. I call them signs because they are indicators that seem packed with implicit meanings without being decipherable as symbols that can be reliably read. Leah said she had been working very hard to get the movements right, but that people would intrude and derail her efforts, such as one nurse who had "hit her with a five." When I inquired into the meaning of the five, Leah pulled back, as though my question alerted her to some danger that was looming. Meaning seemed too precarious to withstand such scrutiny. Such moments require our absolute presence, unbounded by desire or fear. As Davoine and Gaudillière (2004) put it:

> The cognitive stakes are considerable, a prelude to the opening or the closing of the field of *logos*. A disingenuous reply or an embarrassed silence, when adamantly repeated, sends the subject into nonexistence. . . . He exiles himself, falls silent, goes crazy. Instead of speaking *to* him, people speak *of* him, as an aberration. (p. 70)

Most often, our patients are gracious and offer other opportunities. As Leah was telling me about her desire to be able to move properly, she spoke of her dance class and the "five, six . . . " Suddenly, I had some thread of the meaning of "five" for her, which I communicated with excitement. Leah brightened and began to tell me more about the five, linking it to an open hand that might slap you.

Numbers, colors, objects, and events seem so laden with meaning that it is hard to explore them, and yet meaning is everywhere, as she moves from association to association, becoming lucid and then retreating into more highly symbolized and abstract speech patterns that have idiosyncratic rather than consensual meanings. At times, she seems better able to let me into her world, whereas at others my questions seem dangerous, as though they would expose secrets best kept private.

Leah's responses to subtle shadings in one Rorschach card reveal how even modest arousal can result in feelings of bodily disintegration and an inability to determine what is coming from inside or out. "When I see it," she says, "it reminds me of a throat. It kind of makes me want to look at it and apply it to parts of my body . . . [moves her hands to her own throat and applies pressure]. If I put compression on it, would it work better? I don't know. That's what I was wondering . . . "

This tension, and the vulnerability it marks, makes even small decisions difficult. Leah experiences her equilibrium as so precarious that she finds the thought of taking antipsychotic medication particularly terrifying. She describes it as "going unconscious. . . . I feel like I can't even swallow . . . like it's all dark." This fear of being swallowed by a darkness so deep she might drown in it keeps her at an impasse in relation to recommendations that she try these medications. The danger of being taken over by other's demands feels so pressing that she fends off the idea without really being able to imagine in what ways these medications might actually be helpful to her.

If we think of Bion's (1977) ideas regarding *attacks on linking*, we can perhaps better recognize the bits and fragments of current and past history that Leah offers. Her distress is such that these bits are so interspersed with dream and fantasy that it is difficult to separate or catalog the pieces. Rather, we are left with a dialogue in which conscious and unconscious co-exist, interwoven into the type of fabric that has become Leah's own daydream nightmare from which she cannot escape. If we take seriously the isolation and alienation that imprisons Leah in her solitary universe, then our best course would seem to be to try to enter her world as best we can.

From that perspective, I try to understand her in her own context, to build a story in which the threads make sufficient sense that she can find a path that sustains her, rather than being so idiosyncratic and overcontrolled that any intrusion disrupts her and sends her reeling. I try to create a space that might allow her to settle into her own thoughts and report about *her* universe, so that we can imagine a way to survive the disarray and move towards a more coherent and integrated order that won't be so easily crumbled.

Leah begins to find anchors, and to tell me how she uses them: "when I don't want to take the medication, and I think I'm just going to be ok, my Dad reminds me of the SWAT team." This guidepost helps Leah remember how real it was when she was in Atlanta, trying to get rid of the bar codes, being attacked and ambushed by whatever was firing at her from every direction. It is a lived and living moment for her. As she covers her head with both arms and ducks as she talks, past, future, and fantasy seem to commingle in her being. "It's not enough to have the words!" she tells me. She needs to feel it in her body, from which she cuts herself off, desperately trying to find the lightness of being she was able to attain during her anorectic days.

It is easy to wish, along with Leah, for a magical solution to her problems, such as the medication prescribed by current medical standards, or the more elaborate solutions Leah prescribes for herself. And yet, I hear her telling me very clearly that medication does not offer salvation from the troubles that plague her. She says: "But the Geodon, I felt really sick—I was walking around outside barefoot, I thought I was in mourning because I thought my parents died, when I started taking Geodon."

"So, that really made things much worse?" I say.

"Yeah, every time. Except it doesn't have increments, voice side effects—when I don't get the voices—but it wasn't any better. . . . It's probably helpful to my doctor. . . . I hate the smell of it. . . . I feel like there's another thing I want to tell you about my grandma. Every time she'd come to the door she'd always sit like this. She had two bathrooms and one had a rug like a hook rug almost, one was blue and one was red. So that was my mom's mom. And I just wonder if . . . I don't think my grandmom was mentally ill, I think, I wonder if I was just destined to have this issue . . ."

Leah moves away from medication, the realm of doctors, and back towards considering the signs and symbols from her own life, desperately trying to fit them together into a picture that makes sense. I try to join her in this effort, to build a story in which her symptoms are seen as reasonable attempts to solve a problem that no one has been able to help her with.

When she tells me her theory that what is really wrong with her is a learning disability, I agree that there has been ongoing difficulty putting information together to help her confront the obstacles she faced. Even her mother can join in this particular conversation. Freed from the fear of being blamed, the mother can recall times when Leah's difficulties integrating information had come to the fore but then had receded as issues without Leah really finding any assistance. In a meeting with Leah and her parents, I offer the family a model in which very bright young people can be uneven in their learning so that deficits can hide without being constructively addressed, resulting in greater and greater gaps as time goes by. In this model, neither Leah nor her parents are blamed for the dilemma they are in, and seem better able to join together to address some of the pragmatics of their current situation.

Perhaps the most difficult task for me is the one the family has explicitly charged me with: to offer a diagnosis that helps the family to organize their understanding of Leah's ongoing difficulties in a way that points towards potential resolutions. My answer to their question is one that Leah both offers and disavows. In a recent treatment center, she found herself on a ward with psychotic individuals and felt relieved—though also frightened—to be among people whose struggles were so similar to her own. In reading Jamison's (1995) book *An Unquiet Mind*, she is similarly calmed and frightened by what she discovers there.

Although the diagnosis of schizophrenia is the one most descriptive of her symptoms, I realize that the term carries baggage. And so, I give it carefully, knowing that the family has clung to diagnoses such as bipolar and schizoaffective as though to a life raft. And yet, those diagnoses do not truly speak to the actual problems that Leah has been having. As I point to the prevalence of cognitive symptoms over mood dysregulation, Leah and her parents fight to reimpose the mood aspect, affirming their belief that I am giving Leah a diagnosis that has no hope or future; I am imposing a psychic death sentence. To the contrary, I say, this diagnosis points to the types of difficulties in processing and integrating information Leah might have to address as she tries to build a viable and satisfying life for herself.

Leah has known that she is living in a psychotic universe and is so frightened of what this might mean that she tends to retreat and wall herself up further within that prison. In acknowledging the extent of her difficulties, and also believing in her capacity to face them and work with them, I invite Leah to rejoin the rest of humanity, rather than accepting her belief that she would have to *look* or *be* different in order to find a foothold. The little child who was bullied so mercilessly that not-eating became a way of being sufficiently light to float through her life without the burdens of disdain and isolation she had been carrying—that little child can perhaps stand aside from the elaborate chains of ritualized behaviors and cosmic connections in which she has armed herself. At that point, she can perhaps begin to acknowledge the pain as an integrated part of her past rather than an irresolvable circuit she moves through repeatedly, relentlessly, in the magical hope of finally breaking through into that other alternative dimension in which failure is *not* inevitable.

When social forces eliminate the subject, narrating the life story becomes a way of affirming not merely one's being but also one's essential humanity (Davoine & Gaudillière, 2004). Through her attempts at repair, Leah tries to eliminate herself as the flawed or unacceptable subject, to find the rhythm or pattern that might invite her back into a shared common humanity in which she is *not* constantly at risk of being rejected and discarded. In our work, I try to reintroduce her as the subject in her own drama that is unfolding. Crucial to this effort is our ability to hold both the wanted and unwanted elements so that she might learn to accept and integrate them into a story that is both coherent and congruent.

Leah is fortunate that her parents have found treatment for her in a place where her meanings can be marked and held. In stark contrast to this story in which we can find hope of a better future, however, we can see how difficult it can be for individuals with fewer resources to find sufficient respectful ongoing human engagement through which to negotiate some way to be themselves and survive in their social world. As ideas about treatment become increasingly skewed towards ideas about efficiency that neglect the importance of human connections, we run the risk of overlooking exactly how vital those human connections can be (Charles, 2009).

For those standing at the margins of society, if the extent of their distress goes unacknowledged, they are led further and further into despair. The lack of recognition of the very real dilemmas they are encountering further pulls away from the ability to be respectful of the struggle and of whatever resources they do have that they might more effectively bring to bear. At that point, there is the increased risk of failing to resist the oppressive aspects of the mental health system, and to accept one's designation as fundamentally impaired, in a way that overrides and erases one's subjectivity.

Chronicity seems to be, in part, a function of "care" giving systems that fail to support the individual's needs for autonomy and respectful assistance. Disrespect, particularly when we are feeling isolated and vulnerable, can distort and silence us in ways that erase us as subjective beings. How, then, can the therapists engage with people who are in deep trouble in ways that are respectful of them as individuals and also of the very deep trouble they are in? This is a complicated question that can only be answered if one has very clear ideas about one's role as a therapist and the real limits that are attendant to that role.

At its best, in the analytic process we become the witness who can both empathically enter the experience and also remain separate. Quoting once again from Felman (1995): "The narrator herself does not know any longer who she was except *through her testimony. . . .* In itself, the knowledge *does not exist,* it can only *happen* through the testimony: it cannot be separated from it" (p. 53). From this perspective, it is only through the process of narrativization that the subject emerges. For the traumatized individual, finding sufficient space within which to encounter herself and bring together the bits and fragments that have remained unlinked is a precondition for that process of narrativization to begin.

So it is for Leah, who brings into the consulting room a question she has been asking for a very long time: "is it possible to order my experience in such a way that I, as a unique subject, can go on living?" We both hope that the answers she discovers in our work will be in the affirmative; that I can keep in mind her needs, feelings, hopes, and fears sufficiently that we can work together to help her become more adept at living her life. If not, we are faced with that other dire alternative, in which I become one more person who speaks *over* her in my urgency to "be helpful," and loses her in the process.

Chapter Eleven

Meetings at the Edge

When we work with individuals who struggle with psychosis, it is particularly important to have respect for the ways in which our patients speak to us of the unspeakable. As we have seen, trauma can rupture language, so that whatever has become unspeakable may manifest through sign, symbol, or psychotic language. Traumatic discourse is experienced as alien, a story often told implicitly through symptoms best heard through the sensory registers of the less conscious mind. Our resistance to encountering such devastation invites us to distance from precisely those individuals most in need of affirming common human connections. In working with such an individual, it may be difficult to directly negotiate the terms of engagement. Rather, the therapist is called upon to enter into the universe of the other; to learn to speak their language. This process entails our ability to accept the "signs" that are markers of meaning that have not yet been integrated sufficiently to be useful as symbols, so that we can begin to make meanings together. As a way of illustrating this interactive process, I will present the case of a young woman who had been designated psychotic and had come to the limits of what medication and traditional psychotherapy could offer. She came to me asking a question regarding whether or not I might be able to meet her halfway rather than insisting that she engage only in my way, on my terms. My willingness to step outside of conventional practice—and enter into this woman's universe—allowed for the elaboration of important nodes of meaning. Recognizing together the signs and symbols of the negative entities and energy fields through which emotional and relational complexities were marked and negotiated helped this young woman to build her internal and external resources in sufficient fashion to be able to move forward in very pragmatic ways in her life.

I grew up in an era when psychosis was romanticized, when creativity and craziness intermingled and the lines were often blurred. I spent a good part of my adulthood living in Native American territory and in Santa Fe, where mysticism and spirituality are embodied in ways that are often disparaged in North American culture. Books and films such as *I Never Promised You a Rose Garden* (Greenberg, 1964) pulled us into vicarious encounters with our own demons, and those of us who could find ourselves in those stories were tantalized by the often fuzzy lines between fantasy, creativity, and madness. Our music spoke to the intensity of our despair, as in "Fire and Rain" (Taylor, 1970), and also to our difficulties in knowing what or whom to trust, in a world in which vested interests and blind spots skewed vision. In a society in which the fabric was being stretched and the boundaries dimmed, many of us played with the edges of societal prescriptions and inhibitions, whether through political action or by testing the edges of perception through explorations via drugs or spiritual practice. For many, the edges became blurred, including at times the lines between madness and sanity.

I think I am interested in psychosis because it marks trauma in a particular kind of way that also points to *creative potential* that is being thwarted. Having run into obstacles in my own life, where other people's descriptions became barriers that were impossible to penetrate, I am very attuned to ways in which labels can become barriers rather than providing useful structural frames. I also know how easily whatever seems unacceptable can become invisible, as we resist further dysregulating our fragile constructions by bumping up against expectable resistance. Traumatic encounters resist being integrated into memory so that it is often the *gap* that marks meaning in a story that is told and untold at the same time. In this chapter, I will focus on the elusive nature of meaning: how apparent incoherence can come together into remarkably cogent speech when there is a respectful ear upon which the words can register, and also how easily a story can become dislodged in the hands of an unempathic observer.

To illustrate the dilemma, I will talk about my work with a young woman who has been designated "psychotic" and who, after 8 years of intensive inpatient treatment, has been able move out into the larger world. Joan is certain that, if not for the empathic engagement afforded her in this treatment, she would have been labeled schizophrenic and medicated, managed, and ultimately relegated to the back wards of a less user-friendly institution. This young woman has struggled mightily to locate herself within the social fabric of her society, eventually achieving a balance that includes the idiosyncratic ways in which she has organized social and affective meanings, but also recognizes the social structures inhabited by those around her. Having lived in many cultures, including Native American culture and the various alternative realities coexisting in Santa Fe, I was in a useful position from which to hear what she was saying without resisting so much that she could not find anchors in my consulting room.

In counterpoint, I would like to also touch on some of what we have learned in our psychosis study, where we have been trying to get to know our subjects by listening to interviews of patients who have been designated psychotic talking about their experiences of treatment (Charles, October 9, 2009; Charles, Clemence, Newman, & O'Loughlin, 2011). Through our research, we have been able to recognize how tenuous meaning can be, and how easily engagement can be subverted if the interviewer is not sufficiently sensitive and responsive to the other person. One individual may demand a great deal of interpersonal distance, and may only be able to talk in abstract terms, whereas another may demand a great deal of intimacy. Either may be unable to engage in conversation without first setting up the rules of engagement.

I will begin with an interview, taken from the Follow-Along Study at the Austen Riggs Center, in which the subject presented as incoherent and the interviewer pulled for coherency. The interview takes place 15 years ago, with a 21-year-old woman who had been struggling for some time. She has dropped out of college, and has been at Austen Riggs for 3 months, having been admitted in the context of worsening depression and suicidal ideation. At the beginning of the interview, her eyes are averted. She seems depressed, and her speech is slow, halting, fragmented, and difficult to follow. The interviewer prompts a great deal, leaning forward as though trying to make contact. After a few minutes, "Cara" describes being "equally distant from—distanced—from both my parents." The interviewer responds, thoughtfully: "It's almost a poetic phrase, equidistant, equidistant—from both my parents. Is that true emotionally?"

This is the first place where we see the interviewer coming forward, trying to engage the person behind the halting speech. He seems to be responding to the same thing *I* am hearing as I listen to Cara's speech, which is a certain way of organizing her thoughts that points to a real intelligence behind the apparent incoherence. As the interview proceeds, we then see the interviewer doing battle with Cara's own self-dismissal, as he pushes beyond the labels she seems to be trying on for size. We see him very actively trying to find the person, to get to the experience underneath the diagnostic terms that merely mark aspects of psychopathology.

She begins: "I thought I had a borderline personality disorder for a long time—I guess. But I think that's just a . . . something they slap on you when they can't diagnose you."

"What's your own personal diagnosis of yourself?" asks the interviewer.

"I don't know. I thought I was manic depressive for a long time, but . . . and I do have mood swings that are . . . rapid type of . . . but apparently . . . I . . . I had no idea, really, what was wrong. I mean I knew I was suffering from depression, obviously a major depression, but I learned here that I have a schizotypal personality disorder. So . . . I don't know, I guess that's chronic borderline personality disorder."

The interviewer intervenes again, creating a space between the label and her experience: Is it useful, he asks, "does that make sense to you, that label?"

She responds that some aspects seem to fit, and then he asks her to clarify her previous reference to something "psychotic."

"Do you want examples of my psychosis?" she asks.

"Or, do you think of yourself as using sort of psychotic-like . . ." he counters.

Taking his cues, Cara then moves away from the labels and begins to describe her experiences with spirit guides, which go back to her childhood. These depictions are very rich and she clearly has found them to be useful in helping her navigate through her life.

At several points, she wavers, moving back into a confusion between her own language of "my spirit guide" and this other language of psychosis. "My thoughts are bizarre, and my beliefs were—are—kind of bizarre. . . . It's hard because I'm studying Shamanism and a lot of the voices that I hear—or was hearing—are part of that . . . I have spirit guides which give me a lot of insight . . . to myself and others . . . and, my—it's hard to explain—I feel like lately they're inaudible."

Then, a bit further on, Cara says: "I don't think lately, I . . . I don't know enough to judge but . . . whether . . . you know, I'm ok or not. Um, but . . . he would often be fighting with me against my dark side, which . . . ah . . . is hard to explain. I guess my dark side's part of me . . ."

The interviewer moves in again, saying "How does this . . ."

"The dark side," says Cara.

"This particular spirit guide," counters the interviewer, inviting her to talk about the voices, joining in *her* depiction, saying: "How does this particular spirit guide join in the fight, how does he help you fight against the dark side?"

"Well, my journeys are pretty visual," she replies. "Sometimes it's . . . I mean physical fighting, sometimes it's . . . he's a black panther-like creature. . . and sometimes it's more mental, like just remembering that in the medicine area—a place you go to, journey to with these entities—is all faith, and I'm all powerful in that sense. I was neglecting to remember that at one point, and it was just getting me to say, 'Leave this area to . . . to the dark side.'"

"He's a mentor and that's basically I guess why he wants me to call him Sensei. I have another spirit guide who just shows me pictures of tattoos on her hands and her chest, that—well, for instance, my friend is having problems at college, and I said that I'd journey for her, and so I did and one of my lessons—Sensei was teaching me a lesson in trust. . . . I have this other spirit guide at hand who doesn't talk—I call her 'mother' because she's a nun; she's kind of a ghost—she has the tattoos on her hands and chest. And she showed me a tattoo, Sensei kept forcing me to look, look, and, um, finally I saw a tattoo of this picture, it was moving, and it was a birch tree with a limb coming out towards me, and it was a squirrel running down the limb, and it had something in its mouth, and it jumped off and flew down to the ground. And I realized what was in its mouth was a flower, and it put it in the ground, and it fell over, so the squirrel ran away and came back with a bunch of pebbles in its mouth and built a wall around the flower, and the flower stood up, but it suffocated and died.

"And so I had no idea what this was telling me, and Sensei kept saying, you know, trust it. And I hadn't spoken to my friend, who I was journeying for, in a week or so, and when I called her on the phone and told her about, you know, this image that I got, she said, "It's significant already because last night my friends and I were all going around deciding what animals we would be, and this one particular friend who she was having a problem with, everyone decided that that friend would be a flying squirrel. So it all made sense to *her*. So, I mean, that's kind of how powerful, how deeply connected we are."

At a certain point, the interviewer subtly but very explicitly moves against a pathological model, as he characterizes her experience by pointing, not to the possibility that Cara's shamanic encounters are a function of pathological defense but rather: "Do you have to feel good, or well enough, to journey?"

He makes a similar move when Cara talks about having threatened to jump off a balcony. "In order to die?" he repeats, "or in order to fly. Sounds like a funny question, but you mentioned jumping off the balcony was . . . did it involved death or sort of liberation?"

"Um, probably liberation through death," she says. "Or revenge. Maybe it was just constant torment being in that house."

At that point, Cara has moved away from an incoherent narrative, in which she describes herself in terms of psychiatric diagnoses, and into a reflective, complicated exploration of factors that might be implicated in her current distress. Eventually, she comes back to what matters most to her: relationships and music, reporting that during her stay at Riggs she had come to a turning point in terms of committing herself to living. When asked about this turning point, she says it came from reading a book called *Shamanic Wisdom* that helped her realize "how screwed up some of my thoughts were." At the end of the interview, when asked how it had been for her, Cara replies:

"It was fine. I was dreading it, but . . . like I said, I feel very inarticulate and very stupid, and very . . . unsure and confused about everything that's going on, so . . ."

In watching this interview, as researchers, we are taken by how profoundly vulnerable an individual in trouble can be when they find themselves in the hands of authoritative others who in some ways have the power of psychic life and death in a given moment. Perhaps the most important lesson that we have learned from this research is the importance of speaking up in support of the importance of validation, recognition, and the human connection in our dealing with those in distress.

We also can use these data to inform our work with patients who do not fit prescribed norms and yet may have their own ways of organizing and accommodating to life's difficulties. So, now, shifting back to my patient: when I met her, Joan was 23 years old and had been at Riggs since just turning 17. She had been pleased with her previous therapist until they hit a stumbling point they could not get around. As far as I could tell, Joan needed to be able to communicate in her own language and find someone who was willing to try to bridge the gap rather than overriding her and insisting that she speak in their tongue. Joan's language was not so far afield from ways of organizing reality that were very familiar to me as someone who had spent many years in Santa Fe. And so, when her new psychiatrist approached me to ask "Is Joan psychotic?" I replied that she had her own way of organizing reality that seemed to work quite well for her. So, if the question was "is Joan psychotic in a way that we should be worrying about and trying to manage?" then I thought the answer was "no." This seemed enough for the lovely young psychiatrist I work with, and we all went on from there.

Joan was beginning her work with me after five years of intensive psychoanalytic psychotherapy had reached an impasse. She was hurt, angry, and confused, lamenting the loss of this therapist who had been so helpful to her as she found her way back from an isolating madness that had been truly terrible. Joan's way of organizing the universe was clearly unconventional, and yet seemed to be accurate to her experience and to be useful to her as she tried to find her way towards a more satisfying existence. I had the sense that, in choosing to end her previous treatment, Joan was taking a stand for her own need for individuation from the "parent" with whom she had successfully negotiated previous developmental challenges. Now, however, she had no particular model for how this new relationship might proceed aside from whatever confidence rested on information she had gleaned from a close friend who had previously been in treatment with me. His ability to trust me seemed to mark for Joan the possibility that I might be trustworthy during times when no trust existed, and she felt utterly and terribly lost and alone.

Our preliminary work together, while Joan was still inpatient, was supported by a treatment team made up of individuals who were able to help me to tolerate the ebbs and storms of working with Joan, as she came up against her own questions that led her back to the point where her reality had collapsed over a decade ago. She was initially not certain that any of us could weather this storm, and yet, our willingness to try and our ability to maintain some ego integrity in the face of these storms *and also* have her in mind as a complex person with a great deal of integrity helped us to persist together.

Part of what was difficult in this work was that Joan needed me to believe in her and in the validity of her experience. I, in turn, could accept that she has such experience, and could believe it is meaningful, but at times I would have no direct experience of the events that I would mark as metaphor and that she experienced as terrible realities. How we could have in mind that they might be both; how to be respectful of the differences between us and of the value in having two different views—of bi-nocular vision—to bring to bear on complex problems, without diminishing or defacing either is an ongoing challenge.

Sitting, for example, with Joan as she told me of the nuclear explosion that needed to happen, and of her fear that I would not be up to the challenge, I could only tell her of my belief that I would still be there in the wake of the explosion, and that she would still be there as well. Taking seriously her experience while also registering my own as different was at times enraging or obfuscating but ultimately gave an intensity and a vitality to our meeting that felt to each of us as though we had truly survived an explosion of major proportions. Perhaps, I said to her, the explosions had to do with speaking difficult truths and not running away from them. We could each find our own edge in that particular challenge, as we came up against the edges of what we could and could not tolerate without feeling at risk of imminent collapse and fragmentation.

Joan told me her own history of feeling like an alien who has had to try to learn how to engage with human beings. The isolation and despair were profound, as was the extent of her dilemma. By the time I met her, this issue of being an alien had become a bit more remote; perhaps she had been an alien in a past life, she told me. Perhaps that might explain how remote and alienated she had always felt from other human beings. By the time we met, the difficulty was marked by the negative entities that she could locate in specific parts of her body. Here, she would show me, with both hands at her left pelvis, there is a negative entity that feeds on her anger, expanding the difficulties and attacking her with them. Joan was searching for a way to grapple with these forces that held her in thrall, and I tried to make sense of what she was telling me. From my own perspective, I could resonate to the intuitive wisdom of Joan's recognition that her own emotions were implicated in the hold these entities had on her.

We struggled to find ways to meet one another; she in her world; I in mine. At times, it felt to me that she needed me to be her in order that she not feel alone and annihilated by my presence. And yet, as much as I might try to embrace her reality, I am not her and do not share her reality. This space between us at times would feel impossible, as though the world would break apart in the face of such impossible distance between us. I would feel as though I was being asked something impossible and all I could do was to try to survive the debacle. In that survival, we did manage to find one another, and to pick up the pieces. In such moments, I would literally discover how fundamentally meaning had become fractured and fragmented, as I heard her story of what had happened between us. I would sit silently, trying to set aside my own story sufficiently to be able to take in her experience without annihilating it by superimposing my own, even in my mind.

For me, this experience seemed to echo the fundamental struggle Joan was engaged in, as she fought out with me her right (and thus the possibility) to have her own mind in relation to another mind that is not destroyed by and does not seek to destroy hers. Over time, I could see how she was also playing out this dilemma with the healer she visits regularly, who offers a more potent understanding than she could find with me, an understanding more in line with Joan's own language and world view. This healer unhooks the "cords" Joan's mother has hooked into her, thus separating Joan from her mother's impossible demands and accusations. This process leaves her a bit freer to feel her own feelings and work them through, and to practice the healing techniques she has been learning. As Joan begins to bring these practices into our sessions, I have the sense that she is learning self-regulation through her meditation and energy work. Over time, I come to believe that it is critically important for this young woman whose mother was not empathically attuned to be able to work on these self-regulatory processes in the presence of another person who *can* remain empathically attuned as she reports to me about her thoughts, feelings, and experiences.

Through this process of learning and internalizing self-regulatory functions, Joan has been able to confront some of the terrible emotions that had been locked away. Over time, with great and often painful effort, she was able to begin to confront first, her anger, and then, more terribly, her fear. These efforts have afforded us difficult moments in which we are confronted by the need to somehow bridge a chasm that feels unmanageable. In turn, these confrontations have given her greater equilibrium from which to continue to fight to build a viable life. We have discovered that it seems to be enough that I am willing to support Joan's right to find her own way. She no longer insists that I must know or believe exactly what she knows or believes in order for us to be able to work together. As she has learned to better tolerate having two people in the room with different thoughts and feelings, she feels less annihilated by this inevitable otherness. Being able to tolerate this type of interpersonal tension has enabled Joan to push past some of the constraints she had felt in her other relationships. She began to demand respect for her needs and feelings rather than necessarily capitulating to the other as the price of connection. Her developing self-regard has helped her to set limits even when she is heartsick at the thought of losing the relationship. In the process, she develops more highly textured ideas regarding what matters to her in her close relationships such that she can invest in those relationships where real consideration, respect, depth, and intimacy prevail.

Joan has not only been able to get through a semester at college without being so overwhelmed that she needs to drop her classes, she has begun to really shine through her hard work and very fine intellect, and is able to enjoy her successes. She was also able to discharge from the institution that had been her home and refuge for 8 long years. Watching Joan finding her bearings in the outside world was somewhat like watching someone face the light after living her life in a dark cave. Her equilibrium was shaken, but she was able to find her way and to include the disparate and motley group of resources that she had gathered along the way, her therapist, her social worker, her prescriber, her friends, and perhaps most importantly, the Reiki Master who supported Joan in believing in her own powers in ways that helped this young woman to learn sufficient self-regulation to be capable of finding her way, even in this odd universe of 21st century America.

To end, I would like to note that in this young woman's case, we can see how diagnosis can usefully determine treatment, as in the psychotherapy and medications that greatly assisted Joan in her early efforts to fight her way back from the terrible place in which she found herself in mid-adolescence. Over time, however, she could notice, for example, that the drugs that had been useful were now making her feel groggy and unable to think clearly. I can recall the first moment when Joan noted, with some amazement, the fact that she was feeling groggy after having ingested a dose of medication that was thirty times less than she had previously taken regularly. Over time, she learned *not* to marvel when a tiny dose of such a substance now made her so groggy she was almost unable to function. She learned to track her own well-being and to actively advocate for her needs as she saw them. This type of recognition, in the context of a respectful therapeutic engagement, helped Joan to assist her service providers in recognizing changes in Joan and responding accordingly.

Joan has now been in outpatient treatment for over a year. At times, we marvel together at how far she has come. Even during hard times, she is better able to keep or regain her equilibrium and she is building a life for herself that contains both pleasure and achievement. Recently, her psychiatrist became concerned that she might be seeing early signs of tardive dyskenisia and, together, Joan and her doctor developed a plan for slowly titrating down the relatively low dose of antipsychotic that is the one medication on which Joan still relies. Although Joan is somewhat anxious over taking on this challenge earlier than anticipated, her prescriber is quite certain that Joan is, indeed, ready for this event.

Joan entered into treatment with me because she had come to the limits of what conventional psychoanalytic therapy seemed to offer. I am, indeed, both a psychologist and a psychoanalyst, and use my training in my work with Joan. But I also take seriously the charge that brought this young woman into my office, desperately hoping to find a professional who was willing to meet her halfway; to learn her language, to treat her with respect, and to try to help her to work through the problems that she most hoped to solve. We have each worked hard to understand—and sometimes to tolerate—the experience and the language of the other. We continue to meet at that wonderful and sometimes terrifying edge, grateful to be able to count on the other person's kindness and persistence, and also grateful to have been able to travel this territory together.

Epilogue

In the consulting room, we try to create an environment in which people can do something that has hitherto not proved possible. Doing the impossible is no easy challenge, and yet, that is what we have come to accomplish. When something has been shattered that has foreclosed development, moving on is problematic at best. When something of value has been lost, moving forward feels like closing a door and leaving that something behind forever. This type of letting go can feel like one more rupture and can seem unendurable.

Too much trauma impedes our resilience and makes it difficult to play. And yet, finding new solutions to old problems requires that we play with ideas and possibilities, try them on for size, and imagine our way into a future that is less constrained than the past. Being in the presence of someone who invites us to do the impossible—to play—can seem not only impossible but even assaultive. For the therapist, how we build the foundations on which play can occur is the challenge, and it is always a new challenge. We never entirely solve this problem. We can only become more accustomed to facing it.

For me, theory has provided ideas to play with when I am feeling stuck. These ideas help me to imagine ways out of the impossible dilemmas I find myself in with my patients. And so, in this volume, I have offered you some of the ideas I have found most helpful, with the hope that you will find them useful as well. Perhaps more important, I offer you the idea that theory is what gets us through the difficult times we need to be able to survive in order to reach the point at which the other person can become more present in the room and truly enter into the work with us. Once that transition is accomplished, we need to be able to embrace the work as it unfolds. At that point, we should be wary when theory begins to take center stage, lest it represent our own defense against the, at times, terrible intimacy of engaging in this work together.

I hope that the offerings in this volume will serve as constructive companions rather than obstructive forces. The purpose of theory is to encourage reflective function, not to discourage it. In psychoanalytic psychotherapy, we need to be able to have access to both conscious and unconscious resources and, ultimately, it is our ability to play with whatever bits of data we encounter that facilitates our patients' abilities to encounter their own complexity as a challenge rather than a curse. At times, this work can feel as though we are playing precariously on the head of a pin but we also know that we have a heritage of fellow players who recognized the hazards and offered us metaphors and other conceptual tools. These resources can help to hold us as we hold open a space in which our patients can puzzle through the dilemmas that brought them to our doors. It is an odd but very rewarding job we do, one in which prescriptions close down possibilities and faith matters. Ultimately, each patient takes us on a journey neither of us can predict, and each therapist must discover his or her own path. I wish you increasing faith in your own efforts as you proceed along your path.

References

Akhtar, S. (1995). A third individuation: Immigration, identity, and the psychoanalytic process. *Journal of the American Psychoanalytic Association*, 43: 1051–1084.

Allen, J. G., Fonagy, P., & Bateman, A. (2008). *Mentalizing in Clinical Practice*. Arlington, VA: American Psychiatric Publishing.

Amador, X. F., Strauss, D. H., Yale, S. A., Flaum, M. H., & Gorman, J. M. (1993). Assessment of insight in psychosis. *American Journal of Psychiatry*, 150: 873–879.

Andreason, N. C. (2007). DSM and the death of phenomenology in America: An example of unintended consequences. *Schizophrenia Bulletin*, 33: 108–112.

Apollon, W., Bergeron, D., & Cantin, L. (2002), *After Lacan: Clinical Practice and the Subject of the Unconscious*, R. Hughes & K. R. Malone (Eds.). Albany: SUNY Press.

Apprey, M. (1993). The African-American experience: Forced migration and the transgenerational trauma. *Mind and Human Interaction*, 4: 70–75.

Bauman, Z. (1993). *Postmodern Ethics*. Oxford, England: Blackwell.

Bentolila, D. (2007). Trauma and the failure to mourn: A Lacanian perspective on serious acting-out and passage into action. Presented at the XVIII Annual IFPE Conference, Toronto, Canada, October 19–21.

Benveniste, P. S., Papouchis, N., Allen, R., & Hurvich, M. (1998). Rorschach assessment of annihilation anxiety and ego functioning. *Psychoanalytic Psychology*, 15: 536–566.

Bion, W. R. (1967a). *Second Thoughts: Selected Papers on Psycho-Analysis*. Northvale, NJ: Jason Aronson.

Bion, W. R. (1967b). Notes on memory and desire. *Psychoanalytic Forum*, 2: 3.

Bion, W. R. (1967c). Attacks on linking. In *Second Thoughts: Selected Papers on Psycho-Analysis*, pp. 93–109. Northvale, NJ: Jason Aronson.

Bion, W. R. (1977). *Seven Servants*. New York: Jason Aronson.

Bion, W. R. (1977/1989). The grid. In *Two Papers: the Grid and Caesura*, pp. 3–33. London: Karnac.

Bion, W. R. (1987). Emotional turbulence. In *Clinical Seminars and Four Papers*, F. Bion (Ed.). Abingdon: Fleetwood.

Bion, W. R. (1990). *Brazilian Lectures*. New York: Karnac.

Bion, W. R. (1992). *Cogitations*, F. Bion (Ed.). London: Karnac.

Buber, M. (1958). *I and Thou*, R. G. Smith (Trans.). New York: Scribner.

Cantin, L. (2002). The trauma of Language. In Apollon, W., Bergeron, D., & Cantin, L. *After Lacan: Clinical Practice and the Subject of the Unconscious*, R. Hughes & K. R. Malone (Eds.), pp. 35–47. Albany: SUNY Press.

Caruth, C. (1991). Unclaimed experience: Trauma and the possibility of history. *Yale French Studies*, 79: 181–192.

Charles, M. (1998). On wondering: Creating openings into the analytic space. *Journal of Melanie Klein and Object Relations*, 16: 367–387.

Charles, M. (2000). The intergenerational transmission of unresolved mourning: Personal, familial and cultural factors. *Samiksa: Journal of the Indian Psychoanalytical Society*, 54: 65–80.

Charles, M. (2001a). The outsider. *Free Associations*, 8(4:48): 625–652.

Charles, M. (2001b). Reflections on creativity: The "intruder" as mystic OR Reconciliation with the mother/self. *Free Associations*, 9(1:49): 119–151.

Charles, M. (2001c). Assimilating difference: Traumatic effects of prejudice. *Samiska: Journal of the Indian Psychoanalytical Society*, 55: 15–27.

Charles, M. (2002a). Bion's grid: A tool for transformation. *Journal of the American Academy of Psychoanalysis*, 30: 429–445.

Charles, M. (2002b). *Patterns: Building Blocks of Experience*. Hillsdale, NJ: Analytic Press.

Charles, M. (2004a). *Learning From Experience: A Guidebook for Clinicians*. Hillsdale, NJ: Analytic Press.

Charles, M. (2004b). *Constructing Realities: Transformations through Myth and Metaphor*. New York: Rodopi.

Charles, M. (2005). Reparation and Redemption: Nightmare and Memory in D. M. Thomas' *Pictures at an Exhibition* and in a clinical case. *Free Associations*. Available at www.psychoanalysis-and-therapy.com/articles/whatsnew/html.

Charles, M. (2006). Silent scream: The cost of crucifixion—Working with a patient with an eating disorder. *Journal of the American Academy of Psychoanalysis and Dynamic Psychiatry*, 34: 261–285.

Charles, M. (2006b). Precious illusions: Re-constructing realities. In J. Mills (Ed.), *Other Banalities: Exploring the Legacy of Melanie Klein*, pp. 77–104. New York: Routledge.

Charles, M. (2007). The insidious stretching of the envelope: Coping with disregulation, demands, and other assaults on the analytic mind. *The Round Robin*, 22: 5–6, 22–24.

Charles, M. (2008). A view from Riggs: Treatment resistance and patient authority: VIII. System pressures, ethics, and autonomy. *Journal of the American Academy of Psychoanalysis and Dynamic Psychiatry*, 36: 547–560.

Charles, M. (2009). Psychosis and the social link: Fighting chronicity through human connections. *Bulletin of the Michigan Psychoanalytic Council*, 5: 33–44.

Charles, M. (October 9, 2009). *Telling Trauma*. Presentation at panel *Listening to the Dis-Ease of Psychosis*, ISPS-US Annual Meeting, Rockville, MD.

Charles, M. (2011). System pressures, ethics, and autonomy. In E. Plakun (Ed.), *Treatment Resistance and Patient Authority: The Austen Riggs Reader*, pp. 121–135. New York: Norton.

Charles, M., & Clemence, J. (2010). Self-destructive uses of ECT. Unpublished Manuscript.

Charles, M., Clemence, J., Newman, G., & O'Loughlin, M. (2009). Listening to the other: The psychotic patient's experience of psychotherapy. *Psychosis: Psychological, Social, and Integrative Approaches*, 1(S1): S110–111.

Charles, M., Clemence, J., Newman, G., & O'Loughlin, M. (January, 2010). Pathways to psychosis: Psychosis, identity, and connection. Poster at the Winter Meeting of the American Psychoanalytic Association, New York, NY.

Charles, M., Clemence, J., Newman, G., & O'Loughlin, M. (2011). Listening to the Dis-Ease of Psychosis: Preliminary Reports from an Interdisciplinary Research Study. (Chapter under review).

Charles, M., & Telis, K. (2009). Pattern as inspiration and mode of communication in the works of Van Gogh. *American Journal of Psychoanalysis*, 69: 238–262.

Davoine, F., & Gaudillière, J.-M. (2004). *History Beyond Trauma: Whereof One Cannot Speak, Thereof One Cannot Stay Silent*, S. Fairfield (Trans.). New York: Other Press.

Felman, S. (1987). *Jacques Lacan and the Adventure of Insight*. Cambridge, MA: Harvard University Press.

Felman, S. (1995). Education and crisis, or the vicissitudes of teaching. In C. Caruth (Ed.), *Trauma: Explorations in Memory*, pp. 13–60. Baltimore: Johns Hopkins University Press.

Greenberg, J. (1964). *I Never Promised You a Rose Garden*. New York: Holt, Rinehart & Winston.

Grotstein, J. S. (2000). *Who Is the Dreamer Who Dreams the Dream? A Study of Psychic Presences*. Northvale, NJ: Analytic Press.

Grotstein, J. S. (2009a). *But at the Same Time and on Another Level . . . , Volume I: Psychoanalytic Theory and Technique in the Kleinian/Bionian Mode*. London: Karnac.

Grotstein, J. S. (2009b). *But at the Same Time and on Another Level . . . , Volume II: Clinical Applications in the Kleinian/Bionian Mode*. London: Karnac.

Jamison, K. R. (1995). *An Unquiet Mind*. New York: Knopf.

Joseph, B. (1985). Transference: The total situation. *International Journal of Psycho-Analysis*, 66: 447–454.

Klein, M. (1930). The importance of symbol-formation in the development of the ego. In *Love, Guilt and Reparation and Other Works, 1921–1945*, pp. 219–232. London: Hogarth Press, 1981.

Klein, M. (1946). Notes on some schizoid mechanisms. In *Envy and Gratitude and Other Works, 1946–1963*, pp. 1–24. New York: Delacorte, 1975.

Klein, M. (1957). Envy and gratitude. In *Envy and Gratitude and Other Works, 1946–1963*, pp. 176–234. New York: Delacorte, 1975.

Knapp, S., Berman, J., Gottlieb, M., & Handelsman, M. M. (2007). When law and ethics collide: What should psychologists do? *Professional Psychology: Research and Practice*, 38: 54–59.

Knapp, S., & Vandecreek, L. (2007). Balancing respect for autonomy with competing values with the use of principle-based ethics. *Psychotherapy: Theory, Research, Practice, Training*, 44: 397–404.

Kristeva, J. (1986). Revolution in poetic language. In T. Moi (Ed.), *The Kristeva Reader*, pp. 89–136. New York: Columbia University Press.

Lacan, J. (1962–1963), *Le Séminaire, Livre X: L'Angoisse* [The Seminar, Book X: Anxiety], J.-A. Miller (Ed.). Paris: Seuil.

Lacan, J. (1972–1973). *The Seminar of Jacques Lacan, Book XX*, J.-A. Miller (Ed.), B. Fink (Trans.). New York: Norton, 1998.

Lacan, J. (1977a). The function and field of speech and language in psychoanalysis. In *Écrits: A Selection*, A. Sheridan (Trans.), pp. 30–113. New York: Norton.

Lacan, J. (1977b). Presence of the analyst. In *Écrits: A Selection*, A. Sheridan (Trans.), pp. 123–135. New York: Norton.

Lacan, J. (1977c). On a question preliminary to any possible treatment of psychosis. In *Écrits: A Selection*, A. Sheridan (Trans.), pp. 178–231. New York: Norton.

Lacan, J. (1978). *The Four Fundamental Concepts of Psycho-Analysis*, A. Sheridan (Trans.). New York: Norton.

Lacan, J. (1978a). The partial drive and its circuit. In *The Four Fundamental Concepts of Psycho-Analysis*, A. Sheridan (Trans.), pp. 174–186. New York: Norton.

Lacan, J. (1978b). The subject and the other: alienation. In *The Four Fundamental Concepts of Psycho-Analysis*. A. Sheridan (Trans.), pp. 203–215. New York: Norton.

Lacan, J. (1978c). The subject and the other: Alienation. In *The Four Fundamental Concepts of Psycho-Analysis*. A. Sheridan (Trans.), pp. 203–215. New York: Norton.

Lacan, J. (1978d). The subject and the other: aphanasis. In *The Four Fundamental Concepts of Psycho-Analysis*. A. Sheridan (Trans.), pp. 216–229. New York: Norton.

Lacan, J. (1988). *The Seminar of Jacques Lacan: Book I: Freud's Papers on Technique, 1953–1954*. J-A. Miller (Ed.), J. Forrester (Trans.), New York: Norton.

Lacan, J. (1993). *The Seminar of Jacques Lacan, Book III: The Psychoses, 1955–1956*, J.-A. Miller (Ed.), R. Grigg (Trans.). New York: Norton.

LaCapra, D. (1999). Trauma, Absence, Loss. *Critical Inquiry*, 25: 696–727.

Lysaker, P. H., Roe, D., & Yanos, P. T. (2007). Toward understanding the insight paradox: Internalized stigma moderates the association between insight and social functioning, hope, and self-esteem among people with schizophrenia spectrum disorders. *Schizophrenia Bulletin*, 33: 192–199.

Matte-Blanco, I. (1975). *The Unconscious as Infinite Sets: An Essay in Bi-Logic.* London: Duckworth.

Mayes, L., Fonagy, P., & Target, M. (2007). *Developmental Science and Psychoanalysis: Integration and Innovation. Developments in Psychoanalysis.* London: Karnac.

McDougall, J. (1980). *Plea for a Measure of Abnormality.* New York: International Universities Press.

McWilliams, N. (2005). Preserving our humanity as therapists. *Psychotherapy: Theory, Research, Practice, Training,* 42: 139–151.

Mintz, D., & Belnap, B. (2006). A view from Riggs: Treatment resistance and patient authority—III. What is psychodynamic psychopharmacology? An approach to pharmacological treatment resistance. *Journal of the American Academy of Psychoanalysis & Dynamic Psychiatry,* 34: 581–601.

Morgan, C., & Fisher, H. (2007). Environmental factors in schizophrenia: Childhood trauma—A critical review. *Schizophrenia Bulletin,* 33: 3–10.

Muller, J. (2007). A view from Riggs: Treatment resistance and patient authority—IV: Why the pair needs the Third. *Journal of the American Academy of Psychoanalysis and Dynamic Psychiatry,* 35: 221–241.

Novick, J., & Novick, K. K. (1996). *Fearful Symmetry: The Development and Treatment of Sadomasochism.* Northvale, NJ: Jason Aronson.

Parsons, M. (1986). Suddenly finding it really matters. The paradox of the analyst's non-attachment. *International Journal of Psychoanalysis,* 67: 475–488.

Peterson, D. R. (2004). Science, scientism, and professional responsibility. *Clinical Psychology: Science and Practice,* 11: 196–210.

Racker, H. (1968). *Transference and Counter-Transference.* New York: International Universities Press.

Read, J., van Os, J., Morrison, A. P., & Ross, C. A. (2005). Childhood trauma, psychosis and schizophrenia: A literature review with theoretical and clinical implications. *Acta Psychiatrica Scandinavica,* 112: 330–350.

Ritsher, J. B., & Phelan, J. C. (2004). Internalized stigma predicts erosion of morale among psychiatric patients. *Psychiatry Research,* 129: 257–265.

Schafer, R. (1997). *The Contemporary Kleinians of London.* Madison, CT: International Universities Press.

Schreier, A., et al. (2009). Prospective study of peer victimization in childhood and psychotic symptoms in a nonclinical population at age 12 years. *Archives of General Psychiatry,* 66: 527–536.

Schwandt, M. L., Lindell, S. G., Sjöberg, R. L., Chisholm, K. L., Higley, J. D., Suomi, S. J., Heilig, M., & Barr, C. S. (2010). Gene-environment interactions and response to social intrusion in male and female rhesus macaques. *Biological Psychiatry,* 67: 323–330.

Segal, H. (1957). Notes on symbol formation. *International Journal of Psycho-Analysis,* 38: 391–397.

Shapiro, E. R., & Carr, A. W. (1991). *Lost in Familiar Places: Creating New Connections Between the Individual and Society.* New Haven: Yale University Press.

Shils, E. (1997). *The Virtue of Civility: Selected Essays on Liberalism, Tradition, and Civil Society,* S. Grosby, Ed. Indianapolis: Liberty Fund.

Stern, D. N. (1985). *The Interpersonal World of the Infant: A View from Psychoanalysis and Developmental Psychology.* New York: Basic Books.

Taylor, J. (1970). Fire and rain. On *Sweet Baby James* (record). Warner Bros.

Tomkins, S. S. (1962). *Affect, Imagery, Consciousness—Volume I. The Positive Affects.* New York: Springer.

Tomkins, S. S. (1963). *Affect, Imagery, Consciousness—Volume II. The Negative Affects.* New York: Springer.

Unamuno, M. de. (1921). *Tragic Sense of Life,* J. E. Crawford (Trans.). New York: Dover, 1954.

Westen, D., Novotny, C. M., & Thompson-Brenner, H. (2004). The empirical status of empirically supported psychotherapies: Assumptions, findings, and reporting in controlled clinical trials. *Psychological Bulletin,* 130: 631–663.

Whitaker, R. (2002). *Mad in America: Bad Science, Bad Medicine, and the Enduring Mistreatment of the Mentally Ill.* Cambridge, MA: Perseus.

Whitaker, R. (2010). *Anatomy of an Epidemic: Magic Bullets, Psychiatric Drugs, and the Astonishing Rise of Mental Illness in America.* New York: Crown.

Winnicott, D. W. (1963/1989). Fear of breakdown. In *Psycho-Analytic Explorations*, pp. 87–95. New York: Routledge.

Winnicott, D. W. (1965). *The Maturational Processes and the Facilitating Environment: Studies in the Theory of Emotional Development.* New York: International Universities Press.

Winnicott, D. W. (1971). *Playing and Reality.* New York: Routledge.

Index

About the Author

Marilyn Charles is a staff psychologist at the Austen Riggs Center and a psychoanalyst in private practice in Stockbridge and Richmond, Massachusetts. An adjunct professor of clinical psychology at Michigan State University and faculty at several psychoanalytic institutes, she also serves on the editorial boards of many psychoanalytic journals. Marilyn has presented her work nationally and internationally and has published over 60 papers and numerous book chapters. *Working with Trauma: Lessons from Bion and Lacan* is her fourth book. Previously published are *Patterns: Building Blocks of Experience* (2002), *Constructing Realities: Transformations through Myth and Metaphor* (2004) and *Learning from Experience: A Guidebook for Clinicians* (2004).

As the co-chair of the Association for the Psychoanalysis of Culture and Society (APCS) and of the APA Division 39 Early Career Committee, she supports psychoanalytic training, outreach, and research initiatives, and has spent a significant part of her professional life actively engaged in mentoring and promoting community involvement for those in the helping professions. Her primary research interests are creativity and psychosis. She is the co-founder of the Austen Riggs Psychosis Research Study, looking intensively at the narratives of individuals who have been labeled 'psychotic' to explore treatment experiences and outcomes from the patients' perspectives. She is currently working towards a multi-site project that will use interviews to examine developmental antecedents and treatment experiences of individuals who struggle with psychosis.

Marilyn's interest in understanding the creative process has included the study of nonverbal communicative aspects of pattern, tracing, for example, how prosodies of feelings become translated into line and color, and investigating these issues in relation to the works of artists and writers. She has worked extensively with individuals experiencing creative blocks. As creativity requires an ability to move into primary process thinking and return from it, creative individuals often appear psychotic according to projective assessment techniques, and there are no reliable Rorschach indices to accurately assess and differentiate creativity from psychosis. To this end, Marilyn is currently engaged in research using responses from the Rorschach inkblot test to determine what constellation of factors indicate creativity and which indicate psychosis.

An artist and poet, herself, Marilyn has exhibited her work in various settings. Her latest solo exhibition, titled "Fragments," featured her collages and occurred in July 2009 at the George Mason University Gallery.